Patricia Zukowski
and Anne Bello, Editors

The *Anthology* Editorial Board:
Hazel Gedikli
Bükem Reitmayer
Shastri Akella
Dina Al Qassar
Joseph Crescente

The Student Writing Anthology

2017–2018

University of Massachusetts Amherst
Writing Program

macmillan learning
curriculum solutions

10 9 8 7 6 5 4 3 2 1

ISBN 978-0-7380-9328-4

Macmillan Learning Curriculum Solutions
14903 Pilot Drive
Plymouth, MI 48170
www.macmillanlearning.com

Dingo 9328-4 F17

Sustainability
Hayden-McNeil's standard paper stock uses a minimum of 30% post-consumer waste. We offer higher % options by request, including a 100% recycled stock. Additionally, Hayden-McNeil Custom Digital provides authors with the opportunity to convert print products to a digital format. Hayden-McNeil is part of a larger sustainability initiative through Macmillan Learning. Visit http://sustainability.macmillan.com to learn more.

bedford/st. martin's • hayden-mcneil
w.h. freeman • worth publishers

Table of Contents

Part 1: Writing from and across Borders: Essays from *Basic Writing*

Part 2: Writing from and across Contexts: Essays from *College Writing*

Table of Contents

Introduction

It is a hot Tuesday afternoon, and the first day of my College Writing *class. As I enter the compact classroom, I think to myself that it will just be like one of my high school writing classes that strictly focused on grammar and how to form persuasive arguments. I am confident that my soon-to-be classmates have similar thoughts. I arrive early just to be certain that I am in the right place. After finding a seat at the front, and placing the required books on my desk, I wait. Minutes later, it is 1:00 pm. Class is now in session.*

—Amrow Hegazy, "Growth"

Amrow Hegazy describes an experience shared by all the writers in this book and likely by many of its readers: the first day of a first-year writing course at the University of Massachusetts Amherst. Perhaps your class began on a frosty Monday at 9:05 am; perhaps you are taking *Basic Writing*; perhaps you arrived a few minutes late, trying to navigate your way around campus. But you arrived, and like Hegazy, you carry your own expectations of what a writing course will be like.

This book can show you the potential for what college writing can do, and as Hegazy found, that might be very different from what you were expecting.

***

This 40th edition of the *Student Writing Anthology* continues the Writing Program's decades-long tradition of publishing and circulating student work. This tradition grows out of a belief that students are writers and that their work should be shared. Indeed, an earlier edition of the *Anthology* would have been one of the "required books" on Hegazy's desk; this text is required for all sections of Englwrit 111: *Basic Writing* and Englwrit 112: *College Writing*.

Most students come to UMass Amherst well-versed in high school genres: they can write thesis-driven arguments; they have compiled extensive research papers; they are experts in producing essays for standardized tests. In *Basic* and *College Writing*, students begin to produce writing that engages with the world in new, exciting ways. These classes are not "strictly focused on grammar and how to form persuasive arguments," and the writing in this volume reflects that. If you have only written in contexts where the use of "I" is forbidden and introductory paragraphs *must* end in a thesis statement, the essays here will open up different possibilities for how to organize an essay, develop a line of inquiry, and engage an audience.

As you read through this book, you will get a sense of how *Basic Writing* and *College Writing* are different. The essays in Part I come from *Basic Writing* courses, and as you will see, they take up questions of United States diversity. *Basic Writing* is a reading- and writing-intensive course that fulfills a United States diversity general education requirement and is based on the theme of borders. The essays in Part II come from *College Writing* courses; *College Writing* is a rhetorically-oriented, process-based writing course that fulfills UMass Amherst's first-year writing general education requirement. The essays in the *College Writing* section showcase a range of genres, and they take up a diverse assortment of topics, from working in a bakery to the social pressures surrounding happiness in a student's senior year of high school to the environmental impacts of poultry production.

While you may notice some differences among the essays in the two sections—the *Basic Writing* essays frequently take up interconnecting themes of language and identity; the *College Writing* essays invoke a variety of audiences and, in the Adding to a Conversation unit especially, bring in outside research—you will also notice that essays from both courses incorporate personal experience and value student knowledge and insight. In both courses, students are encouraged to put their knowledge into dialogue with other writers' ideas. Students are also invited to discover their own purposes for writing and to explore different options for structure, style, and even language itself.

There are a few key elements of *Basic* and *College Writing* that you won't be able to see in these essays. Both courses are process-based, which means students take their writing through a drafting cycle, beginning with generative writing (or brainstorming) and then moving through a series of revisions. None of the essays in this book started out in the form you see them now. They began as rough ideas and initial drafts and went through multiple iterations through the revision process. They have all gone through an additional round of revision as they were prepared for publication, though we have worked to preserve the distinctiveness of each writer's voice.

The social dimension of writing is also invisible in these pieces. As these writers crafted their essays, they consulted with their peers and worked with their instructors. And as their essays moved to publication, multiple people were involved along the way. Writing Program Assistant Director Patricia Zukowski, who has been deeply involved with the *Anthology* throughout its history, led a committee of graduate student instructors—Shastri Akella, Dina Al Qassar, Joseph Crescente, Hazel Gedikli, and Bükem Reitmayer—through the lengthy process of selecting texts for the *College Writing* section. Robin Garabedian, Marlene Perez, and Lauren Silber offered their insights in compiling the *Basic Writing* section. Gedikli and Reitmayer, with early support from Ann Ward, provided extensive editorial support for this book, from collecting permissions and copyediting texts to checking citations and helping recognize student work at the annual Celebration of Writing. Writing Program Director Rebecca Dingo and Assistant Director Peggy Woods consulted on selections and citations, and office staff members Heidi Terault and Becky Blajda provided logistical support. Erin Southward, Erica Lee, Cheri Bowman, and the staff at Hayden-McNeil provided their time and expertise in bringing the book through production. In short, this volume—like most pieces of published writing—represents the work of many people, and to all of them I say, "Thank you."

***

Hegazy concludes his essay with an image of himself at the computer, "hands firmly placed on my keyboard and mouse in my dim-lighted dorm room," writing.

Class is now in session.

What will you write?

–Anne Bello

Part 1

Writing from and across Borders:
Essays from *Basic Writing*

Preface

Turn on the news, and borders seem to be everywhere, from political debates about immigration to stories of migrants fleeing conflict and seeking economic opportunity. But as the essays in this collection show, borders are not just national and physical: they can be intangible markers of difference; they can be seemingly impenetrable barriers to change; and they can be crossed, sometimes easily, sometimes at great cost.

Students in *Basic Writing* spend the semester writing and reading about borders, their many forms, and their often complex implications. Throughout the semester, students work through four main units: Colliding Spaces, which examines physical, spatial, and geographical borders as well as intangible borders; Defining Lines, where the focus shifts to national borders and questions of immigration and assimilation; Interweavings, which considers how culture and identity shape and are shaped by borders; and Unsettled Voices, which explores how language crosses, creates, and challenges borders. As students move through these units, they produce essays that engage with readings and course content in a variety of ways, experimenting with different writing "moves": writing from personal experience; entering into a dialogue with a reading; analyzing a text; and using multiple sources to persuade readers. *Basic Writing* instructors decide which sequences of units and writing moves are the best fit for their classes; during the first unit of the course, one class might be analyzing a text focused on the theme of language, while another class might be writing from personal experience about physical borders. By the end of the semester, all *Basic Writing* students consider the same thematic units and explore the same writing moves, but each class follows a different path to that end.

As a result, the essays in this section do not correspond to specific units the way the essays in the *College Writing* section do. Instead, these essays show a range of possible ways for students to write about—and alongside, in response to, and even against—other texts in the course. For example, Gongtao Yang's and Erica Zheng's essays bear many similarities to each other on the surface level: both authors incorporate personal experience and interact with multiple published texts in essays about accents and identity. Zheng uses sources as points of connection to reflect on personal experience; of one source, she writes, "I could resonate with [the reading] from my own experience." Yang, on the other hand, uses Michael Jones-Correa's essay as a framework for an in-depth examination of accents and belonging. Together, Yang and Zheng demonstrate different approaches students might take even when working on thematically similar topics.

Some of the essays in this section do lend themselves to particular units and particular genres. Aneeswar Bairavasundaram's essay, for instance, is a rhetorical analysis of an essay that speaks directly to the themes of the Unsettled Voices unit. Other essays connect with themes of multiple units. Yue Dai's essay could be read in conjunction with multiple units: the essay considers borders connected to a physical space, Shanghai (Colliding Spaces); discusses the changing status of a particular language, Shanghainese (Unsettled Voices); and reflects on how culture and identity change over time, as groups of insiders and outsiders interact (Interweavings or possibly Defining Lines). And Dai's essay might also be read for its structure or vivid use of sustained metaphors.

Like Dai, many of the writers in this section take up questions of language, but they do so in different ways. José Reyes writes an argument calling for the reform of language education in the United States; Sara MacDonald mentions in passing that "I know that my mother could speak this sort of mystic other language" as she reflects on her relation to her Armenian heritage. Readers will find resonances and common themes among many of the essays, though each writer brings a unique perspective to course content. Before each essay is a short introduction, which suggests how the text might fit into the *Basic Writing* curriculum. These introductions, however, are not meant to limit how these essays might be taken up in the *Basic Writing* classroom; in short, these essays are not meant to be confined within the borders of a particular unit.

These essays do, however, provide content for students to respond *to*. Oshiomah Oyageshio, who uses multiple sources as well as personal experience to persuade readers, ends his essay by asking, "Racism is not dead. Will it ever be?" These essays highlight complex issues and pose difficult questions, pointing to the challenging intellectual work of the course. Just as students in *Basic Writing* are encouraged to write in dialogue with James Baldwin and Amy Tan, they are also invited to engage with the ideas of Oyageshio and of Bairavasundaram, Dai, Lv, MacDonald, Niland, Reyes, Yang, and Zheng.

Rhetorical Analysis of Baldwin's "If Black English Isn't a Language, Then Tell Me, What Is?"

ANEESWAR BAIRAVASUNDARAM

In this textual analysis, Bairavasundaram examines how James Baldwin's tone and word choice create pathos and logos. Pathos and logos are two ways writers can persuade or influence readers. When using pathos, writers appeal to readers' emotions; when using logos, writers use logic, knowledge, and facts to influence readers' responses. Bairavasundaram analyzes how Baldwin's choices as a writer support his argument in favor of Black English.

"*A language comes into existence by means of brutal necessity*" (Baldwin 154–155).

Black English, a language with a majority of Black speakers, represents the dark and oppressive historical past of the United States. In 1979, a prominent figure, James Baldwin, addressed the importance of classifying Black English as a new language and the historic relevance of the language's formation. In his essay, Baldwin also criticizes the ignorant attitude towards Black English and its consequence on the Black community. He ultimately pushes for classifying Black English as a language, which is an important step for social equality.

Baldwin uses aspects of emotion portraying anger when describing a reason why Black English is not considered a language. Baldwin states the white people's dilemma of not being able to "afford to understand [Black English]. This understanding would reveal to [them] too much about [themselves] and smash that mirror before which [they have] been frozen for so long" (155). By stating that white people cannot accept their historic past and Black English's history, he claims that calling Black English a dialect of English is a manner to circumvent the dark past of the United States. In context of the Civil Rights movement, Baldwin suggests that the reason behind the lack of racial equality stems from white peoples' inability to bear their slave-owning past and accept how they are truly viewed in an oppressive view by Blacks.

Baldwin shows his true emotion when describing the white people who disrespect Black English as "*uptight*, middle-class white people, imitating poverty, trying to *get down*" (154). Baldwin's voice dramatically changes from a neutral tone into an angry and serious tone when he mentions white people using but not respecting the Black language, which in turn disrespects the Black culture. The shift of tone signifies what impact white people's ignorance of the Black culture has on Blacks. He indicates that white people do not understand that imitating poverty is much different than true poverty and tries to state that certain terms and phrases have a much deeper meaning (154). He also uses Black language when describing white people's actions such as "trying to *get down.*" By using "Black" terms he assures both his knowledge of the language as well as uses it as a means of giving the true definition of the "Black" terms. In addition, many literary rules applying to foreign languages are used. For example, he writes that it is "late in the day to attempt to penalize black people for having created a language that permits the nation its only glimpse of reality … without which the nation would be even more *whipped* than it is" (154). Baldwin uses sarcasm to explain that Black English's origin stems from the times of slavery and explains how the language symbolizes the United States' dark past. He italicized "*whipped*" to denote the word as if he were including words from another language. The placement of the term from Black English is carefully chosen as it is after Baldwin uses his logos to explain why Black English is a language. By doing so Baldwin slowly causes the readers to go through a logical process and accept Black English as a separate language.

In addition to conveying his emotion to his readers, Baldwin also uses logical statements to enforce his thesis on his target audience. As Baldwin begins to state that Black English should be considered its own language, he begins by making a series of arguments which eventually end by proving his point. Baldwin states that the status of language "has nothing to do with language itself but with the role of language" (153). Baldwin begins by stating the argument that he is trying to prove of what role language plays and how Black English fulfills the roles of a language. Baldwin states facts about Black history and defines language as "[coming] into existence by means of brutal necessity" (154–155). By giving historical facts of Black English's existence, Baldwin lets readers discern whether Black English fulfills the criteria of a language. He also describes the role of language and how it "reveals the private identity [of an individual]" (153), so that to "open your mouth … is (if I may use black English) to 'put your business in the street'" (154). The role of language is described as a marker of identity. Baldwin carefully uses terms from Black English to give an example of how language serves as a classification of identity as well as to cause the readers to relate with personal experiences in dealing with others who speak foreign languages.

Baldwin using logos and pathos causes the reader to accept that Black English is a separate language. Baldwin indicates that when white people ignorantly mock Black English and use disrespectful terms, they are insulting a culture that had gone through decades of being oppressed. Through his sudden anger and shift in tone, Baldwin emphasizes the need for change. Being written post-Civil Rights era shows that political equality is not sufficient enough but also that societal equality is equally as important. Baldwin's overarching concept is that no language or dialect should be made fun of as each language represents a culture and each culture represents the struggles and happiness of a community.

Work Cited

Baldwin, James. "If Black English Isn't a Language, Then Tell Me, What Is?" *Reading and Writing on the Edge*, edited by Deirdre Vinyard et al., Pearson, 2014, pp. 152–155. Mercury Reader.

Inherit Our Precious Pearl

YUE DAI

By reflecting on the changing status of Shanghainese, Dai examines how globalization, culture, identity, and language can intersect, creating and erasing borders. Dai divides the essay into sections but creates cohesion by using recurring metaphors and returning to the idea of "different cognition," the varied perspectives of people who grew up in Shanghai and those who have moved to the city for economic opportunities.

Same Pearl, Different Cognition

Shanghai, oriental pearl inlaid in China, is always considered an international city. Everyone knows the preciousness of a pearl, but only its owner knows its touch: warm, comfortable, feeling of peace, which is worth much more than its price. Most of the people outside can only see Shanghai's prosperity—the high buildings and huge shopping malls—which attract millions of people from different states, different countries. In Shanghai citizens' eyes, tiny cafés located in the peaceful streets are the soul of this beautiful city. They're sweet candies that can comfort a crying child. The cognition difference between Shanghai citizens and external population borders these two groups apart. People from outside bring dynamism, economic benefits, and various cultures into this city. However, Shanghai's own culture seems to be covered by them. Spicy (fast-paced) lifestyle, bitter (hard) works and living... hardly can we taste the sweetness of this city sometimes. Shanghainese, the language used by Shanghai citizens and the highest representation of this city's cultural treasures, is continuously disappearing.

A Childhood Full of Stories

Shanghainese grammar is almost the same as Mandarin. The difference between them is the pronunciation and some specific usage of vocabulary. As a port city, Shanghainese contacted with other languages (especially English) frequently in 1980s and absorbed many usage of them. One of the examples is cement, Shanghainese called si-men-ting, transferred from English pronunciation. Ricksha drivers perhaps are the creator of these words. They hadn't been educated, but they would communicate with foreigners every day. Butter (Ba-tuo), Vaseline (Fei-si-ling), Too bad (Tei-bei)… These easy-understood words for both foreigners and drivers become popular among them. Such pronunciation and interesting stories inside words give Shanghainese unique charms.

My grandparents came to Shanghai when they were young, so they can and are only able to speak Shanghainese fluently. As a result, Shanghainese is our family's "common language." From when I was small, my grandparents always told the origin of Shanghainese words before I went to bed, not Disney fairy tales. Although I could remember few of these, I actually learned how to speak Shanghainese. So before I went to school, this was the language I heard and used most. I even remember that when someone greeted me in Mandarin, I felt uncomfortable in this strange pronunciation. I lived in a Shanghainese world in my early childhood. Borders between Shanghainese and other languages seems impossible, because as I thought, everyone should speak Shanghainese, which is an ordinary fact, until I went to elementary school.

Welcome to Mandarin World

There's a saying: "Enter the school is like entering Beijing."[1] In my elementary school, every mirror had a label above saying: "Please speak Mandarin." The first scene when I saw these labels seems funny: I read these labels loudly in Shanghainese. However, after several days I realized that it's not a joke. Teachers and students were not allowed to speak Shanghainese during classes. There were no classes about history and usage of Shanghainese. It became a "shadow language" behind Mandarin. I forgot what's the feeling when I entered class, but it should be taken for long to change my language using habit. We studied Mandarin pronunciation in Chinese class so the issue wasn't so obvious, but in other classes (like math or science) I sometimes answered questions in Shanghainese without consciousness. "Speak Mandarin! You are breaking class orders!" and, my classmates began laughing (perhaps they thought I looked like showing off myself).

Actually, these unhappy memories didn't last long. The only fact I remembered is that I hadn't spoken Shanghainese in classes any more after grade one. I could understand why Shanghainese was forbidden in classes: many of my classmates and many of the students in my elementary school could not understand Shanghainese. I told myself, *That's ok. I can speak Mandarin in school and Shanghainese at home.* However, the whole city seemed the same as my elementary school, or even worse. Labels became more ridiculous: "Speak

---

1. The origin of Mandarin

Mandarin and be a polite person." There's a period of time that services couldn't speak Shanghainese even if the customers could get it all. Of course, Shanghainese is forbidden in media communication.

Our newspaper, the biggest newspaper in Shanghai called "XinMingWanBao" published an article. Until now, I can remember each word in this article, criticizing Shanghainese: "Most of new Shanghainese (Shanghai people) work in office buildings in Pudong. Especially in LuJiaZui,[2] everyone speaks Mandarin, and speaking Shanghainese is a reflection of uneducated." I couldn't believe that such a brazen author could write such a shameless article that could be published in newspapers. Certainly Shanghainese had protested this article, but we hadn't received any apologies from anyone.

Culture Robbing

It's the time that I realized the seriousness of this issue, felt the strong border between Shanghainese and Mandarin: three-fourths of my classmates couldn't speak Shanghainese, although most of them were from Shanghai. It's hard to hear young people talking in Shanghainese on the street. Only in some old residential area could I hear my homeland's language. This beautiful language was cut and deleted violently among people under the age of 40. This was no different from cutting the future and inheritance of Shanghai's local culture. Our country is generalizing Mandarin in order to achieve a "national unity," but it has also desalinated the language, the culture, history of our city invisibly. In my city, I speak this city's language, but someone said: "Sorry, what did you say?" It's a funny story. But it exists everywhere.

New Shanghainese, those who come from other states to make a living in Shanghai, do contribute to our city's developments indeed. However, some of them don't respect our culture. They hope that Shanghai can be constructed to a world-wide city that everyone can live in without any barrier. More than once, I have seen some of the opinions on website, which is complaining about hearing Shanghainese in public. At that time Shanghai doesn't belong to Shanghainese, but belong to Chinese.

It's the different cognition that leads to borders between two languages, two groups of people. In other words, different cognition is the origin of border and its formation cannot be avoided. Some people said Shanghainese have a characteristic of anti-foreign. However, why should we welcome those who look down on us, on our precious treasure? They consider Shanghai as their gold mine, and we also have rights to protect our living places.

---

2.   The Central Business District in Shanghai

You are brewing up a cup of tea and it is under a heavy fragrance first. After several times brewing this cup of tea, the smell disappears. When you want to find more leaves, there's almost nothing left. Shanghai is like this cup. Every year millions of people are moving in this city. They can speak Mandarin; they can speak their own language; they can speak everything they are accustomed to, except Shanghainese. They are just like the hot water, desalinating our culture time after time. I'm a piece of new, lonely leaf, waiting to be brewed up.

Spread Our Culture, Inherit Our Treasures

Someone brought our lost leaves back. A talk show about Shanghainese and Shanghai culture in 2010 woke the citizens up. This show consists of several lively and interesting stories in the generation of my parents' childhood, which reflects the history as well as the culture of Shanghai. When watching the talk show, my mum ceaselessly talked to me about her childhood and stories behind Shanghainese words. For her, it's a hard but sweet memory she picked up again. For me, it's the inheritance of our culture. Shanghainese, the most essential part of this talk show, revives the identity as a Shanghainese inside every local citizen's heart.

People became aware of the importance of protecting Shanghainese, the original language they should grasp. Various folk organizations stood up to hold activities introducing Shanghai's charming culture, of course using Shanghainese. Many famous drama performers suggest taking protection in Shanghainese so that there can be plenty of young performers to maintain this only kind of artwork using Shanghainese. The movement of citizens works. From 2013, the voice prompts in buses now has three languages: Mandarin, English, and Shanghainese. TV programs began publicizing Shanghai's old drama performer, allowing everyone to discover the fascination of Shanghainese.

For me, talking with classmates or teachers in Shanghainese in my high school was so common and nobody minded it. When I went to visit my elementary school, I couldn't see any labels above the mirrors. My teacher told that some of elementary schools add Shanghainese class once a week, including mine. More and more people around me from other states also ask me about Shanghai's culture and Shanghainese. When I heard "侬好 (nong hao)" (Hello) from their mouth, from more people's mouths, I really felt that I'm living at home, not in my past elementary school.

Compromise or conflicts, even replacement are never the solutions to handle borders, especially which between Shanghainese and Mandarin. Each of them has their own significance to exist. They should coexist with each other equally. We are just trying to let more and more people know the fascination of Shanghainese, to learn more about their homeland's history and culture, and more, to inherit these invaluable treasures to posterity. All of us have an ideal thought in our mind: cognition difference can be erased one day and everyone is able to feel the pearl using their own hands.

Incognizant Border

MENGHUA LV

Drawing on personal experience, Lv explores how language and technology can create borders between generations. Lv uses dialogue and a sustained example to explore how individuals can help—or prevent—others in crossing language borders.

"You didn't answer my texts for a few days. Is the schedule too busy?" said my mother during dinner time. My hand reaching for the apple on the table stiffened for a while, and before I could try to find a proper way to answer her question, she just continued her talking as if it was not a question she wanted answered. "Anyway, just don't stay up too late. It's bad for your health." She started telling me to look after myself once again as same as she told in the texts. Suddenly I felt that the guilt rising in my heart would almost submerge me.

It was two months ago, when some groups on the internet started using "233" to present the means of laughing, because the number "233" presents the 233th emotion, which is laughing on the software. At first it was just some famous bloggers started used "233" to replace "laughing" for fun. After a week, it got more and more popular so that even my friends used this number when texting. It can be even considered as a fashion among young people. Yet when I texted a funny message to my mother and ended it with "233," she got confused and curiously asked me what it meant. It took a while for me to explain the meaning of this number to her.

As the time went on, plenty of new words appeared in the texts among my friends. To catch up with their conversation, I mixed these new words from the Internet in my texts. Sometimes I just subconsciously and mistakenly sent them to my mom, and then she would ask me the meaning of them with great interest. As I tirelessly explained them to her, I began feeling impatient, ignoring her inquiring texts. I asked my friends for help, and many of them thought that it would be easier to set a border between us and our parents than to explain all the new words to them.

Only few among them had the patience to explain all the meanings of the new words and how to use them to their parents. It was at that time I noticed that most young people would separate the language into several parts: one of them is for speaking to parents, and "233" obviously does not belong to this part. I was convinced to do so, and no longer sent texts with the Internet words to my mom. It worked. She did not ask me those questions anymore, which made me feel relaxed for a while. I did not need to bother with the endless texts nor trying to find a proper explanation for her.

Before coming back to home, I was immersed in the easiness of getting rid of the incessant inquiries, being unaware of the existence of the language border between me and my mother. A broad river it is, separating us by the water of words. I can only hear the vague sound of my mother from the other side and talk to her with equally vague sentences.

It was at the dinner on Friday night. My mom said to me proudly about how she explained the meaning of an Internet word to the colleague in her department: "She was so surprising about that because her son in the college never talks those words to her." My lips quirked a little, trying to tell her that the explanation she made was wrong and that she might confuse the meaning of other words with it. But I wasn't hard enough to break apart her joy. "I hope you can teach me more about these internet words," she said, putting on her glasses, squinting her eyes, and starting to read the texts. "I am so happy that you can explain these words to me. I used to teach you how to read when you were young, and now it is you to teach me how to read." The sadness, like a growing seed, besieged my heart with its fine but strong roots. I noticed the border between me and my mother, the border I built to separate me from my beloved, for the first real time. It used to be my mom who taught me how to pronounce the first syllable, how to recognize the first word. She built up a bridge for me to cross the river so that I can get into this world. There is no reason I should be impatient to build a bridge for her.

How amazing the language border is. It brings me and my friends together while it separates me from my mother, as the two sides of the coin. We can hardly judge it by a simple example. The only thing we can assure is that it would continue existing as long as the language exists.

Identities throughout Generations

SARA MACDONALD

Through the use of vivid details, MacDonald sets up a thoughtful reflection on immigration, identity, and generational difference. She brings in Bharati Mukherjee's "Two Ways to Belong in America" to deepen and extend her analysis of her family's experiences with immigration and identity.

My grandmother resides in a rehabilitation center that smells overwhelmingly of cleaning chemicals and day old pot roast. I call her in the mornings and visit her on the weekends that I am home from school. She looks eerie surrounded by white. White walls, white sheets, even her face has lost the color it once held so intensely. I sit at the end of her bed, and she asks me the same question that I hear every time I see her, without exception:

"Do you remember picking strawberries in the backyard with Mez Mama? Oh, she loved you girls."

Mez Mama, the Armenian saying for grandmother, is what my entire family refers to my great grandmother as. I have built up what I'm sure is an imaginary memory of this in my mind from being told the story so often. I envision my sister and I holding Mez Mama's hand, tracing the strawberry bushes that no longer stand in the yard, as she speaks in her native language to us. I hold onto other memories from my childhood in Watertown, the town where a majority of my Armenian family lives. Walking through it all looks something like this:

I am holding a plastic bag under a ladder as my mother drops down grape leaves from my grandmother's cherished grapevine. The leaves, wrapped around a hand-built wooden post, are a jungle in the sky through my small eyes. I am sitting in a kitchen chair that is much too big and covered in too much uncomfortable plastic, trying to roll lamb into these same leaves for one of many traditional Armenian meals. I am laying with photographs spilling onto the floor around me as I look into my family's past life. I am pouting with my sister in the basement of my cousin's house as our relatives speak in a language that we cannot understand. I am curled into my great aunt's lap and she is kissing both of my cheeks, pinching both of my cheeks. She does this over and over, telling me that I am her "cherub." Years later, I find out this means fat little angel.

I feel disconnected from my culture because my mother tried so hard to make sure that she was not defined by it. I think back one year to my mother leaning against the frame of my bedroom door, apologizing to me for the way that she speaks ill of my grandfather. She tells me that her father was always of good faith and good intentions, but he had heavy opinions and strong restrictions. She tells me of the somewhat secluded life she led growing up, how she never felt normal. No sleepovers, clothes that never matched her classmates', and God forbid she date without approval. She often tells my sister and me about her struggling to get permission to go to college, to escape some of the expectations that came along with being so tightly wound into the Armenian culture. Though my mother loves her father infinitely, I think that she associates a lot of her cultural values with him and his overbearing ways. She and her siblings were of the first in their generation to marry outside of the ethnicity. Growing up, it never occurred to me that I was something more than simply American. I knew that my mother's side was different from my father's. I knew that my mother could speak this sort of mystic other language. I knew that sometimes, on holidays especially, I ate food that held a more powerful flavor than what we normally had.

To my family, Mez Mama was magic. I hear about her always. I see my mother go back in time whenever she recalls growing up with her. I think what my family admires the most about her is the way that she continued to gracefully embody all of their Armenian traditions when she came over to America. How she connected them all to a place they could have so easily forgotten and left behind. Just as Mez Mama did, my grandmother clung to her Armenian identity. This is evident in her surroundings and her every mannerism. It is something I pick up on whenever I go for my routine visits. Sometimes her house feels like an entirely different planet than my home. There is a line that starts at my head and ends at my toes, drawn straight down the middle of me, separating my Armenian heritage from my American one.

Similar to my family, Bharati Mukherjee addresses carrying on and living with her native identity and traditions in America in her essay "Two Ways to Belong in America." Mukherjee and her sister, Mira, were born and raised in India and moved to America, where they found themselves going down different paths. Mira got married to an Indian student and still dreams of her home in India. Mukherjee married an American despite her family's customs (45).

Feeling betrayed by the laws targeting legal immigrants, Mira threatens to pick up and go back to India. Mukherjee understands her sister's fears and concerns, but feels less strongly about them. When addressing the issue, Mukherjee writes, "America spoke to me—I married it—I embraced the demotion from expatriate aristocrat to immigrant nobody, surrendering those thousands of years of 'pure culture,' the saris, the delightfully accented English. [Mira] retained them all" (47). Just as my Armenian family came to America and split into different cultural directions down the line of generations, Mukherjee and her sister each created new ways to live with their Indian traditions. Though both of the girls feel connected to their lives in India, their time in America brought a new meaning to each of their identities. Mez Mama and my grandfather, like Mira, stood strong on the grounds of their cultural identity. Skip down a few generations, and my mother leans more towards Mukherjee's mindset. I find myself somewhere in between, without as much of a choice as Mira, Mukherjee, and my relatives had.

Today, I carry around bits of both sides of my family. My mother tells me more and more stories of my grandfather. I make promises to come cook with my grandmother when she returns home from rehab. My mother gives me turquoise rings on special occasions, and we exchange "evil eye" trinkets whenever we come across them. When I am nervous or troubled, I touch them knowing that to most Armenians, they are emblems of good luck and protection.

We choose to belong, or to not belong, to our cultures. We have the ability to cut ties just the same as we do to build new ones and maintain old ones. There is, however, no avoiding our own history. We are a combination of our family's past and our own present and future. Mez Mama decided to hold onto as much as she could of her culture when coming to America, with my grandfather following close in her footsteps. My mother chose to let go of the parts of her Armenian culture that she felt suffocated by and to pick up parts of the American culture that she felt could be a better part of her. Mira felt she would be "happier to live in America as expatriate Indian than as an immigrant American" (48). Mukherjee found herself ready to settle into the American culture while putting less stress on her Indian identity. There is no right or wrong way to adapt to a new home. When immigrants come to a different country, there is no ultimatum of picking one identity over another. I cannot claim to know much about leaving one's culture behind and picking up a new one, but I believe that we are a blend of the cultures that we choose to surround and define ourselves by. Who is to say where the Mukherjee sisters' children may end up, what they will hand down to their children, and their children, and on, and on? Who is to say how much of my Armenian culture will disappear and reappear throughout the generations of my family? We live with and pass on the identities that we choose to, no matter what country we find ourselves in.

Work Cited

Mukherjee, Bharati. "Two Ways to Belong in America." *Reading and Writing on the Edge*, edited by Deirdre Vinyard et al., Pearson, 2014, pp. 44–48. Mercury Reader.

Surviving in the Eye of the Storm

KELLY NILAND

Niland applies James Paul Gee's concepts of primary and secondary Discourses to reflect upon how school has shaped her thinking and her relationship to her family. Gee defines Discourses as "ways of being in the world; they are forms of life which integrate words, acts, values, beliefs, attitudes, and social identities as well as gestures, glances, body positions, and clothes" (6–7). Niland engages with Gee's ideas to add analysis to a vivid account of personal experience.

As I entered my third school of the year I was too shy to show my new fourth grade teacher my crooked grin. I was happy to sit quietly as I looked longingly at my new classmates. Even though I had only been there for three months I missed the friendships I had cultivated in my previous school. My only solace was that I was placed with a foster family I knew and loved. But this would prove to be a short-lived bliss—I would be moved again after three years. I was barely comfortable in my oversized sweatshirts, much less my own skin. I never felt like I belonged in one particular place. However, after years of foster care, I was placed with my aunt when I was thirteen. At the time I thought I would finally be with people I could relate to. This was not the case. Fast forward to my junior year of high school. There are tears streaming down my face as I stand in the corner of the crowded school lobby. My shaky foundation begins to fall apart as my aunt tells me she wants to revoke her guardianship. It was then that I realized the hurricane might never stop.

Neither of my parents graduated from high school. My grandmother is from a rural town in Ireland, where she ended her schooling in the sixth grade. I come from a loving and undereducated family. I am one of the first to go to college with the intent to finish. I've been in school for the majority of my life. In school I was taught very specific ways to treat those around you. This does not mean that every single experience I have had in the public school system has taught me to be a politically correct robot that has no opinion of its own. It's just the social structures built within the school setting have engrained inclusive behaviors in my nature. Not only was I taught inclusiveness from the start, I was also taught to think differently than my parents, and this has only widened the divide that was there before. I often feel like my education has put a barrier between my family and me—a barrier that I didn't want but a barrier I keep reinforcing. My education has allowed me to fit into many different circles, but it has also distanced me from my family.

While my home life was always changing directions like the winds within a hurricane, school was the eye of my storm. When my beloved foster dad was dying from bone cancer, I diverted my sadness into studying sedimentary rocks and rivers. When my brother and I were separated, my English teachers encouraged me to escape into the world of Harry Potter or the poetry of Emily Dickinson. While school is a secondary Discourse by definition (Gee 8), it became the primary Discourse I was never afforded at home. I argue that—because of the circumstances when I was younger—my secondary Discourse has acted as a surrogate primary Discourse. It was not as consistent as living in the same house and town for my childhood but for the most part social expectations in the classroom are uniform throughout Massachusetts. School taught me how to behave, how to treat others, and how to make friends. It taught me empathy, compassion, and humility. It taught me the right way to speak, and it taught me how to think. I've been fortunate enough to have teachers who cared about my thoughts and how I thought them.

Long before the metaphorical hurricane hit my life I only saw the good in my parents. This was my potential for a real primary Discourse (Gee 7). I didn't see their flaws; I only saw their love. I didn't notice how they would treat some people differently than others—I only saw them the way they treated me. But throughout my years of school and my years without them, I started forming my own opinions on subjects they never really delved into, topics ranging from race and gender equality to climate change and the way the American economy works. I was encouraged to think about others in way that my parents do not, and because of that I ended up having views that rivaled those of my parents. My dad, for example, believes climate change is a natural phenomenon that was going to happen with or without human involvement. This is not true, but he doesn't understand. Because of his beliefs I exclude him because I am embarrassed by the way he acts. It's the way my surrogate primary Discourse has affected me.

While the hurricane is long gone, I'm still picking up the pieces. I am creating a better, more educated life for myself while trying to restore my connection with my parents in a way that doesn't dismiss their opinions. I am learning to respect them for who they are, rather than excluding them because they don't think the way I do. It won't take emergency disaster personnel, but it will take time.

Work Cited

Gee, James Paul. "Literacy, Discourse, and Linguistics: Introduction." *Journal of Education*, vol. 171, no. 1, 1989, pp. 5–176. *JSTOR*, www.jstor.org/stable/42743865.

Running in the Same Place

OSHIOMAH OYAGESHIO

After using personal experience to capture the reader's attention, Oyageshio incorporates multiple sources to construct an argument about racism that considers local, national, and digital contexts. Oyageshio resists a tidy conclusion to his essay, instead asking readers to consider the larger, complex questions he raises. Please note that this essay includes an image of graffiti containing a word that Merriam-Webster Online *describes as "perhaps the most offensive and inflammatory racial slur in English."*

A couple of weeks ago, I spent my spring break on the UMass campus. I was on the bus back from the town center, and I got off at the stop closest to the dining commons. I walked to Hampshire Dining Commons. As I entered the building, I was overwhelmed by the number of people here compared to the relatively empty rest of campus, probably because it was the only DC open. I found a seat and I went on to fill my plate with food. Pizza, pasta, dessert—I was hungry. As I sat down, I checked my phone to browse the Yik Yak app. Yik Yak is a social media app where anyone can freely post their thoughts, called "yaks," anonymously, and the viewers can comment, up vote, or down vote on the posted yak. The yaks are often locked to particular locations, such as college campuses. It is used by students as a means of discussion, information, and as an outlet for venting; it's like an anonymous bulletin board.

As I scrolled down through the yaks, one caught my attention. It read, "The black boy in the blue backpack is a thug and should leave Amherst." Let's call this anonymous Yakker, X. To paint a clearer picture…

I am black.

I was wearing a blue backpack.

All sorts of emotions started to flood: anger, confusion, sadness, denial. I clicked on the comments of the yak. Someone asked why he said that. X went on to say, "Someone bumped into him in the bus and he threatened a boy on the bus with a knife." I began to think back to my time on the bus. Did I really do this? Was I possessed by some spirit that made me violently threaten people? Last I checked I'm a pacifist, and I don't usually have the confidence to talk to strangers on the bus, let alone threaten them.

In my denial phase I started to mentally fish for reasons why I wasn't the one in the yak. I recalled my journey from the bus to the dining commons. I was certain there were no other black boys with blue backpacks who rode a bus like me. I started to realize what this situation really was. It was a racially charged statement… *against me*. Why? I rode the bus seated alone, plugged into my headphones. Apparently I'm a thug for doing that. X went out of his or her way to fabricate a false story about me. I looked at my food, and I lost my appetite. My stomach was already filled with knots. I looked around the dining commons. Could X be here? I didn't know. I wasn't comfortable. Paranoia consumed my thoughts. X was lurking behind the shadows, protected by the anonymity of the Internet. X could be someone I see every day, someone I smile at, someone living on my floor. There's no way to know. I checked Yik Yak again so I could take a screenshot of the yak, but it had more than five down votes, so it was deleted. For a moment I was happy that other people felt that his yak was racist but X had already done the damage. I had every right to feel safe and confident eating in the dining commons, but X managed to rip that away from me that afternoon.

What I experienced is called "ethno-stress," as described by Josh Odam, a fellow black UMass student. He describes ethno-stress, in a *Collegian* essay, as "mental and social pressures students of color face while in predominantly white spaces." He writes about this because he has experienced his own version of ethno-stress. Last year, he travelled to Ferguson, Missouri, for a rally following the Michael Brown shooting. Upon his arrival back to his dorm on campus, he saw this graffiti on his door:

Courtesy of Josh Odam/Daily Collegian

He writes about this ordeal in "#WrongDoor: Ethno-stress and Racially Charged Attacks on the UMass Campus." Odam gives an example of ethno-stress as being a minority in a large lecture hall that is primarily white but to add to that having "social and mental pressures" of racist situations like his and mine. He writes that it's these kind of situations where ethno-stress "rears its ugly head." One of the commenters on the article, who goes by "Ed Cutting," makes some interesting points. He writes that the graffiti must have been made in a short time period before Odam arrived because the Residential Assistants wouldn't have allowed that to stay up for so long, deducing that the writer of this may have even known Odam. The miscreant may have known that he was a secretary of diversity for the Student Government Association. Did Odam's credentials make the writer of this uncomfortable, arouse anger, hatred or threat? Probably.

The university held a Town Hall Meeting because of this incident and two other racist vandalism acts that occurred in the student dorms. There were a couple of *Collegian* articles that covered this meeting. In the article, "Racist Vandalism Prompts Emergency Meeting to Discuss Race Relations and Diversity," Catherine Ferris, a *Collegian* reporter, quotes the president of the Muslim Students Association, Elkhansaa Elguenaoui, who spoke in the meeting, as saying, "I think it's time to talk about such a topic. A topic that's so manifested in where we live. We live under an illusion that it's in the past, but it's 2014, and it's still huge. We've pushed it under the rug. It's time to dig it up and deal with it." This comment takes me back to my Yik Yak experience. I remember soon after that experience talking to my friend about this in my dorm. He explained, "[X] is a coward and probably a fat troll. Normal socially acceptable people don't do that. It doesn't matter—just forget about it, man. You're 6'3 and muscular—you can probably take him down." Although I appreciated his sentiment, I got into a heated debate with him. I argued that people that appear to be "normal" can be racist, and I can't just "forget about it." Like Elguenaoui said at the meeting, we need to deal with this. We need to expose what is going on in the shadows and not pretend everything's okay.

I worry that racism and its ignorance will forever exist. I feel it's easier for whites to say things like "Just forget about it," "It's 2015; racism isn't really a thing anymore," or "There's no need to protest in Massachusetts; it's a liberal state." They haven't been in our shoes or faced the prejudice blacks have faced, but they still tell us how we should feel about it. Just to be clear I am not saying all whites think this way. The most offensive statement I've heard regarding this issue was during a discussion in the dorm. My friend (the same one I narrated my Yik Yak incident to) told me that the whole "Black Lives Matter" movement should be altered to "All Lives Matter." We had a verbal argument that spanned three days because of this. In fact we still argue till now. Not only on his opinion on Black Lives Matter but other things like how the society should be more grateful to police officers for the good they do and stop painting cops with a racist brush. I argue that we know the police are good. Nonetheless, it is their job to exhibit fair justice, especially when making arrests, regardless if they think suspects are guilty. It is not a requirement to applaud the police for doing the right thing. Although we can, we don't have to. It is their job.

There has been another instance of ethno-stress I've experienced. There is another social media app called FADE that is similar to Yik Yak. Each post is called a "Fade," and in this app there is a section dedicated for Fades from UMass and Westfield State University (WSU). There was a post, by someone who I will call "L," that read, "Stop the #blacklivesmatter shit. All lives matter. Just stop doing stupid shit and comply with the law." What was even more astounding was that it had 153 up votes. One hundred and fifty three people (and counting) in UMass and WSU agreed that blacks should stop doing "stupid shit" and comply with the law. Don't other races do "stupid shit" as well, or is it that black peoples' "shit" is worse than others? Another question to these people is this: Do you think that us blacks are supremacists and think only our lives matter? Of course we don't, but blacks are the ones that are unjustly gunned down by white police officers. Take the Eric Garner and Michael Brown cases for instance. Whether the victims were criminals or not, they deserved fair treatment especially when they are arrested. We say "Black Lives Matter" because we are hypervigilant and afraid. That slogan is a defense mechanism, and we are condemned by people like L for having such a slogan. Fortunately, it is possible to have chats on FADE, so I instigated a conversation with this person. After I presented these points to L, this was his reply:

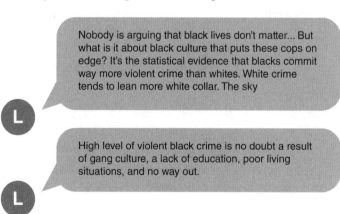

Nobody is arguing that black lives don't matter... But what is it about black culture that puts these cops on edge? It's the statistical evidence that blacks commit way more violent crime than whites. White crime tends to lean more white collar. The sky

High level of violent black crime is no doubt a result of gang culture, a lack of education, poor living situations, and no way out.

> I don't have the answers, man. But I also don't have sympathy for those who break the law. If people would get off of their asses and do something, there wouldn't be a problem. Join the military for christs sake.

> I'd rather have my tax dollars paying for them to serve our country rather than be a drain on it.

©Hayden-McNeil, LLC

I replied:

> How can they join the army when we feel the country hasn't done anything for them? What kind of point is that,

He replied back:

> Everything fine and dandy, I'm not a fucking idiot. ITS A SOURCE OF INCOME

> It's an honorable source of income. When the shit starts flying, you don't think about your country. You think about your brothers and sisters next to you. Loyalty doesn't even have to have anything to do with it. Better to risk your life for your country

> Than drain it in prison.

©Hayden-McNeil, LLC

I'm not really sure what L means by black culture putting cops "on edge." According to an online report "Homicide Trends in the United States, 1980–2008" by the US Department of Justice, blacks accounted for 52.5% of homicide offenders from 1980 to 2008 while whites accounted for 45.3% (Cooper and Smith 3). So is it the 7% disparity in homicide rates that makes cops hypervigilant? L and others like him believe that cops see a black teenager on a street and assume he might be a criminal because of this supposed "black culture." Why can't cops look at Barack Obama or Ben Carson and think that kid on the street may be our future president or the next great brain surgeon?

In my opinion, the "All Lives Matter" argument is very weak. It's just like saying that we should have "masculinists" in addition to feminists, and colleges shouldn't have women's studies departments but only gender studies departments. Just because all genders matter should we also discount the fact that women also have had a history of oppression? If the pro "All Lives Matter" believers think we should start saying "All Genders Matter," we have a greater problem on our hands.

I feel one of the main reasons for this everlasting argument on race occurs because different people have different predisposed mindsets. Are these mindsets because of the color of our skin? Maybe. After I narrated my Yik Yak incident to some of my white friends I got some interesting responses. There was the friend I described earlier, but another one said, "It could have been a joke"; he later on rebuffed his statement after giving it more thought. Why the initial statement, though? Does he believe that we live in a perfect world without racism where X's statement could have been a joke?

Do black people have a shrouded judgement that makes us look like victims in racial situations? Do white people have a predisposed mindset that blacks take racial situations too seriously and feel we always overreact? Does that make everyone prejudiced? Possibly. Maybe racism isn't just black or white (no pun intended). It's like a spectrum and most people fit somewhere along the line.

Over the years there have been great milestones in combating racism in America. I still feel we are somewhat in the same position as we were a century ago only with more civilized dynamics. It has moved from black people being chained and forced to work in farms to cyber hate crimes and ignorance. Obviously those situations are very different but the latter could be viewed as an evolved, less barbaric version of the former. We've gone from physical oppression to socio-economic and psychological subjugation (e.g., ethnostress). In physics, the law of conservation of matter states that energy can neither be created nor destroyed but is converted from one form to another. Maybe the same can be said for racism. Is it going to be in a perpetual state of evolution, or will it end?

Racism is not dead.

Will it ever be?

Works Cited

Cutting, Ed. Comment on "#WrongDoor: Ethno-stress and Racially Charged Attacks on the UMass Campus," by Josh Odam. *Massachusetts Daily Collegian*, 16 Oct. 2014, dailycollegian.com/2014/10/16/wrongdoor-ethno-stress-and-racially-charged-attacks-on-the-umass-campus/#comment-1023135.

Cooper, Alexia, and Erica L. Smith. "Homicide Trends in the United States, 1980–2008." U.S. Bureau of Justice Statistics, U.S. Department of Justice, Nov. 2011, bjs.gov/content/pub/pdf/htus8008.pdf.

Ferris, Catherine. "Racist Vandalism Prompts Emergency Meeting to Discuss Race Relations and Diversity." *Massachusetts Daily Collegian*, 16 Oct. 2014, dailycollegian.com/2014/10/16/racist-vandalism-prompts-emergency-meeting-to-discuss-race-relations-and-diversity/.

Odam, Josh. "#WrongDoor: Ethno-stress and Racially Charged Attacks on the UMass Campus." *Massachusetts Daily Collegian*, 16 Oct. 2014, dailycollegian.com/2014/10/16/wrongdoor-ethno-stress-and-racially-charged-attacks-on-the-umass-campus/.

Just Another Language

JOSÉ E. REYES

Reyes crafts an argument for changing second language instruction, incorporating personal experience with essays by Amy Tan and Maxine Hong Kingston. In addition to describing the process of language acquisition, Reyes sheds light onto the emotional and social dimensions of learning a new language.

It takes approximately three months to learn the basics of a new language. People who are learning Standard American English as a second language face a large number of obstacles. One of these obstacles is evident in Amy Tan's "Mother Tongue," which focuses on the struggles of her mother as an immigrant in America. From personal experiences I know that another obstacle people who are learning Standard American English as a second language in America face is that you are thought of as different and looked down upon. This feeling is shared in Maxine Hong Kingston's "Silence" where she describes the way she felt when she had to speak English in front of other people who spoke proficient Standard American English. People who are learning Standard American English (SAE) as a second language are not given a fair chance and are looked down upon, which affects their self-esteem in a negative way. They are alienated and thought of as different by those who already speak SAE. A way to fix this would be to teach it in a different way, changing the way in which the class is perceived.

Immigrants who speak English as a second language and do not speak perfect SAE are not given a fair chance at many things. Tan's mother is a good example of this happening. Tan explains to the reader how when her mother went to department stores, banks, and restaurants they would "not take her seriously, did not give her good service, pretended not to understand her, or even acted as if they did not hear her" (133). This happened to Tan's mother just because she was speaking with an accent, or speaking "broken" English (132). These people who knew how to speak SAE were purposely alienating Tan's mother simply because of the way she spoke. It got to the point where "when I [Tan] was fifteen, she used to have me call people on the phone to pretend I was she" (133). That way, the same people who were alienating Tan's mother and treating her differently because she was not able to speak SAE the way they were able to would stop treating her differently. The only way Tan's mother was going to be treated equally was if her daughter, who did not speak with an accent, spoke for her. This is a big obstacle which immigrants who do not speak SAE as well as others face almost every day, whereas someone who did speak SAE well would not have to go through this.

The way which Standard American English is taught to students who are learning English as a second language can be degrading and feels like people are looking down upon you. I am someone who learned English as a second language while knowing how to fluently speak Spanish. The third grade is one of the most important years in school. That is where the foundation to properly learn the language is set. Everything builds upon the foundation built in the third grade. I spent my third grade year in the Dominican Republic. I moved to America in the fifth grade and was put in an English Second Language class (ESL). The curriculum of this class consisted of the regular third grade English book. At first I was not bothered with starting to learn English this way. But then when the sixth grade came around and we were still using the same third grade book, I was furious; it was not enough of a challenge. After learning from the same book for one entire school year, I wanted to push myself. I asked the teacher if she was able to teach me from the sixth grade book, and she agreed. I am sure my teacher was not underestimating how smart I was. However, the people who were making the curriculum for the ESL classes were. They did not believe that a sixth grader who is only on his second year of learning English could handle anything above of what a normal third grader could handle. I felt like I was being looked down upon, as if I was not smart enough. It is degrading to think that a sixth grader can only handle the workload of a third grader for two straight years, only because they are learning English as second language.

Another obstacle immigrants who cannot speak proper SAE face is being alienated because of the way they speak. Going through middle school as an immigrant who is still in the process of learning English was not easy. I was constantly picked on because of the way I spoke. One time, in my seventh grade English class, it was my turn to read. The paragraph had words which I wasn't able to pronounce properly. As if they were part of a choir, the whole class burst into laughter when I read the word "character" with the *ch* sounding like the word "chair." Feeling like I was being looked down upon by those in power and having people make fun of the way I spoke affected my self-esteem in a negative way. Kingston also felt this way when she was learning English. In her essay Kingston described how she was embarrassed to speak SAE in front of others because "the same voice came out … bones rubbing jagged against one another" (141). Kingston knew that when she spoke the rest of the kids were going to make fun of her because she was different. It was bringing her self-esteem way down and making her not want to speak. But of course, people like us would have to fight through the obstacles and speak our way out of it. Even if those who spoke SAE the "right way" were still alienating us and making fun of us.

The way that Standard American English is taught to immigrants who are learning it as a second language needs to change. This current way of going from easy to hard in one step is not working. The basics should be taught in an easy to understand way, but the class should get progressively harder. Right now people who are learning English as a second language are being treated as if they were not smart enough to handle hard coursework. English is being treated as if it is some sort of impossible language and the people teaching it cannot challenge those who are learning it. Also, the way it is being perceived needs to change. It would be a lot more comforting if instead of always referring to the class as an "English second language class" to just learning another language. If those who are teaching change the perception of the class, then the rest of the people will follow. I was once guilty of thinking about English as my second language, but now I use it more than Spanish.

Works Cited

Kingston, Maxine Hong. "Silence." Vinyard et al., pp. 137–141.

Tan, Amy. "Mother Tongue." Vinyard et al., pp. 131–136.

Vinyard, Deirdre, et al., editors. *Reading and Writing on the Edge*. Pearson, 2014. Mercury Reader.

Accent and Identity

GONGTAO YANG

Yang integrates personal experience and multiple sources to complicate assumptions about accents and identity. In particular, Yang interrogates what it means to be an "insider" in a community, responding to Michael Jones-Correa's ideas about immigration and perceptions of belonging.

As an international student, I have the chance to see and experience cultures other than the kind that I come from. Due to family reasons, I traveled through China before I came to United States. For the same reason, I have experienced the variety of the way people speak that is caused by geographic reasons even though they speak the same language. People can easily find out that I am not local because of my accent even though I try to speak standard Mandarin. When I came to UMass as an international student, people could easily tell that I am not from here, which is true. As Michael Jones-Correa mentioned in his article, "How Immigrants Are Marked as Outsiders," language is one of the factors that determine whether a person is considered an outsider or an insider. Certainly when people judge whether a person is an insider or an outsider, language is a factor that plays a significant role, but why? Why do people think that way? And more importantly, how is language affecting this matter? Is it always reliable?

The answer to the first question is obviously simple and can be easily comprehended. It is common sense that people from different places have different accents. For instance, people from Southern United Sates tend to speak differently compared to people living at the Canadian border. If people can tell the difference in the way others speak even when they speak the same language, then we can easily imagine that telling that English is a person's first language is easy. For this reason, immigrants are considered outsiders especially those from countries in which English is not first language since they cannot easily erase the accents they have.

By logic, if a person wants to become an "insider" of a society or a community, then this person has to get rid of his/her original accent in order to avoid being labeled as "outsider" when speaking to others. In my own experience, switching accents is far more complicated and miserable than many people think. The first few weeks seemed that nothing significant would happen, but at one point I realized that I had changed. I did not speak the way I used to speak; I found a sense of foreign tone in my voice even when I was speaking Chinese. That feeling can be terrifying and miserable. Fearing that one may lose his identity during the transformation or the process cannot be undone; a person may have some degree of stress caused by this situation. As Ray Gwyn Smith once said, "'Who is to say that robbing a people of its language is less violent than war?'" (qtd. in Anzaldúa 157). It might seem irrelevant to our topic, but it shows that changing the way people speak is a violent and brutal process even the subject in this case is willing to do this.

If changing the way you speak is hard, then why change? Why do some people change it voluntarily, and some people refuse to change? To answer the questions, let's dwell on one of Jones-Correa's theories about how an "outsider" is identified. One of the reasons that immigrants are considered as "outsiders" is immigrants are not considering themselves as part of the community (Jones-Correa). How can they consider themselves a part of a community when others treat them as "outsiders" because they speak differently? People tend to judge even though they do not mean to do so; therefore, during some conversation immigrants might sense that kind of judgment and feel excluded. On one hand, some people might try to get rid of the accent so that they do not need to fear being thought as "outsider"; on the other hand, some may simply withdraw from engaging "insiders" so that they do not need to worry about being judged. Either way will not be an easy path, as Bharati Mukherjee said in her article, the transformation is painful and harsh (48).

As a matter of fact, some people did not realize they are in the process of changing. Most of them can find out by talking to a friend or a family member that know how them well. Then this raises a question, is it always correct? Are the things we discussed so far lies?

It is true that we can find out a lot of information about a person from his accent. But is it always reliable? I would say no. Sometimes a person can adapt a local accent when staying there for a long time. One example of mine is that I adapted some northern accent when I moved to northern China, but I was born and raised in southern part. When I was visiting my home town, my friends told me that I have a strong northern accent, which I did not realize, and it was only a couple of years that I moved away. And this does not just happen to me. I found out that some of my friends at UMass who came to the United States when they were kids all have Cantonese accents, especially those who lived in Cantonese communities. Are they "outsiders"? Almost every one of them would say they are; even though they spend more time in United States than in China, they still picture themselves as Chinese rather than American. So language alone cannot determine whether a person is "insider" or "outsider." If you are not convinced, then let's explore one other extreme case. My cousin who was born in United States and never went to China speaks with some Chinese accent that I think comes from his father, my uncle. He is legally an American, and he thinks he is an American rather than Chinese. He is clearly an "insider," but he still does not speak like an "insider."

All in all, simply judging a person by the accent or the language is not always correct. However, I have to admit it can be used, and it can tell a lot about a person. If people want to become "insiders," they do not have to, but it would be easy if they do adapt local accents. By adapting the local accent, they can make the process of becoming an "insider" easier, since others will not judge them on sight. It is true that accent and language do play a huge role in becoming an "insider," but the whole play still needs to be found by doing so in person.

Works Cited

Anzaldúa, Gloria. "How to Tame a Wild Tongue." Vinyard et al., pp. 156–167.

Jones-Correa, Michael. "How Immigrants Are Marked as Outsiders." *New York Times*, 18 Nov. 2012, www.nytimes.com/roomfor debate/2012/11/15/how-immigrants-come-to-be-seen-as-americans/how-immigrants-are-marked-as-outsiders.

Mukherjee, Bharati. "Two Ways to Belong in America." Vinyard et al., pp. 44–48.

Vinyard, Deirdre, et al., editors. *Reading and Writing on the Edge*. Pearson, 2014. Mercury Reader.

Finding Identity

ERICA ZHENG

National identity, race, politics, and language: Zheng explores all these topics as she reflects upon her changing understanding of her own identity. Zheng incorporates both anecdote and multiple sources as she makes the case that identity is "an ever-changing and fluid concept."

I never had any trouble finding my identity before I was twelve years old. In 2010, at the age of twelve, I moved to the United States. That is when everything changed. My world was turned upside down. Some things I used to believe in almost religiously, such as communism, are perceived as devils by the new people around me. Suddenly, I was lost, lost in another part of the world thousands of miles away from where I called home. It is normal to not know exactly who I was at the age of twelve, but that twelve-year-old me was desperate to define myself in order to feel a sense of belonging in a place where everything was different and unfamiliar.

Before 2010, I was a part of the majority. In a country with 99% of the population being Han Chinese, it was easy for me to blend into any crowd. Everyone in my hometown looks similar in one way or the other. In addition, we all speak the same languages. Then in 2010, the life-changing year of my life, I suddenly became the minority. I still remember the day I landed at John F. Kennedy Airport. It was May 23rd, the first day in the beginning of my new life. Starting that day, I have been surrounded by people who look different, dress differently, and speak different languages. I was exposed to, for the first time in my life, people of other races.

I started school in a diverse community that is half White and half Asian. Even then, I struggled to define myself. People around me, my friends and family members, avoid the topic. In the beginning, I tried to assimilate into the American culture and be American. I learned the customs and the language. I am not a fast learner so I struggled with the English language, especially with speaking English. Just like how Anzaldúa's mother does not want her daughter to speak English with a Mexican accent, my parents said the exact same thing to me (157). They did not want me to have a strong accent when I am speaking English. I did not either because I thought if I speak English the same way as a native-born American, I would feel like I belong. I almost felt pressured to reach my parents' and my own expectations of perfecting my accent.

It was not until much later that I realized I should be proud of my accent. I was at work taking orders from a family of tourists from England. The family was friendly so we chit-chatted while they were waiting for their drinks. During our conversation, the father asked me if I was from Singapore because of my accent. I laughed and responded, "No, I am Chinese." It felt so natural to me. In that moment, I realized I am actually proud of my origins. I also understood that my accent is a part of who I am. It represents my history, and it is such a huge part of my life story. Trying to obtain an American accent is equivalent to attempting to hide who I am.

I speak English with an accent because Mandarin is my first language and the English language was introduced to me much later in my life. Instead of hiding my background as a native Chinese speaker, I have learned to embrace the fact that I am proud to be able to speak two languages. In Min-Zhan Lu's article "From Silence to Words: Writing as Struggle," she tells her story of growing up in the midst of two conflicting worlds: "the world of home, dominated by the ideology of the Western humanistic tradition, and the world of society dominated by Mao Tse-tung's Marxism" (437). She said, "The conflict ultimately helped me to grow as a reader and a writer" (437), in which I could resonate with from my own experience. The conflict of growing up in the Chinese culture and the American culture, of speaking two distinctly different languages, has allowed me to grow as an open-minded individual.

Accents are a representation of diversity. People from different places speak differently. I have always known that I speak English with an accent. But I never even thought that I have an accent when I am speaking Mandarin because I was surrounded by people who have the same accent. A college friend once commented on my accent because she had trouble understanding a word that I said. She started asking me to pronounce other Chinese words. I then found that I have been pronouncing simple words wrong my entire life and some of my friends' names wrong the entire time I knew them. I have always known that I do not speak perfect standard Mandarin. However, somehow I never became aware that I have an accent speaking my native language until someone else with a different accent pointed it out. When I finally made that connection, I realize how proud I am of my hometown. I also speak the local dialect, Fu Zhou dialect, which is very difficult to learn for outsiders because it is drastically different from Mandarin. The locals mix up the dialect and Mandarin when they speak. That is how they talk and how I learned to talk, which is why to this day, I still cannot distinguish my r's and l's amongst many other sounds I cannot pronounce correctly. In a way, Fu Zhou dialect gives me my unique accent, and I love it because what it says about who I am. People would ask what city are you from, and I can proudly say Fu Zhou. Fu Zhou is where I grew up and where I developed my values. It is a part of my identity.

Just like how I consider accents are an inseparable part of my identity, politics are also a huge part of who I am. Before moving to the US, communism was an unchallenged concept. But here, many people critique communism as if it is a cult. I felt isolated when I heard others talking badly about communism. Even though I do not know exactly what communism is, I was raised to love communism and to think that communism is the best form of government. Going to school here challenges that. I had to learn to accept that not everyone believes in communism. Most people believe what they are raised to believe and never challenged anything. I was raised up to praise communism, and they were raised up to despise it. That was okay. I learned to accept that it is okay to believe in different things. Politics says something about me and my personal values. Although I do not belong to any political party now, I have my own set of political beliefs and have developed opinions on political topics. I agree with Mukherjee's statement that "the price that the immigrant willingly pays, and that the exile avoids, is the trauma of self-transformation" (48). From how she worded this sentence, she sees self-transformation as a negative thing. However, I enjoy this process of self-transformation. I have been able to broaden my eyes and explore what is out there.

I am still finding my identity. To me, identity is an ever-changing and fluid concept. Exposure to different perspectives and ideas shapes my identity. I am also constantly exposed to different things in college, and I will be later on when I graduate from college and start my career. Just as I am developing my political opinions, I am also developing my identity.

Works Cited

Anzaldúa, Gloria. "How to Tame a Wild Tongue." Vinyard et al., pp. 156–167.

Lu, Min-Zhan. "From Silence to Words: Writing as Struggle." *College English*, vol. 49, no. 4, Apr. 1987, pp. 437–448. *JSTOR*, www.jstor.org/stable/377860.

Mukherjee, Bharati. "Two Ways to Belong in America." Vinyard et al., pp. 44–48.

Vinyard, Deirdre, et al., editors. *Reading and Writing on the Edge*. Pearson, 2014. Mercury Reader.

Part 2

Writing from and
across Contexts:
Essays from
College Writing

Inquiring into Self

Preface

College Writing begins by asking students to examine the "self," or one of our many selves, as a text in a unit called "Inquiring into Self." The self, after all, is a text that absolutely must be read and re-read with great attentiveness, for it shapes how we understand, interpret, and interact with the world. Using the writing process (generative writing and reading, composing and revising, giving and receiving feedback to and from fellow writers, and editing), students are asked to discover new insights about how their contexts have shaped them. The challenge is to read their stories and bodies as histories and to begin to re-see themselves through the lenses of social contexts—e.g., towns, churches, athletic teams, ethnic communities, and more. Here, students write meaningfully about their own lives. The following essays illustrate this inquiry into self and invite a close audience of classmates to engage with each writer's experiences and critical reflections.

Life Lessons from the Bakery

LAURA BOWLES

Set in small-town Massachusetts, Bowles's essay shows that there is a certain kind of magic in the everyday, in the routine, that begs to be reflected on. Bowles maintains a balance between specificity of detail and analysis that is at once close and deep: offering a close reading of experiences alongside sentences spent on a few selected moments.

On a sleepy one-way street in the seaside city of Salem, Massachusetts, sits a small, unassuming bakery that is known for serving the crustiest sourdough breads, the flakiest pastries, and perhaps the most delicious coffee you'll ever find. Its interior is cozy and warm, with furnishings made of reclaimed wood sourced from old church pews and big windows that let in the soft yellow sunlight. The bakery is an attractive respite for hungry patrons and weary travellers, but despite its delicious offerings and local media praise, it has remained largely undiscovered by Salem residents and visitors for one reason: the bakery is notoriously difficult to locate. In fact, I almost never found it myself.

It was late summer, and I should have been preparing to return to Amherst for my final year of college. However, instead of spending the last days of summer packing my belongings and saying "see you later" to my hometown friends as we moved back to our separate schools, I found myself perusing Salem's streets, looking for any bank that might hire me for a teller position. I had withdrawn from college the semester before, and although I felt little enthusiasm for becoming a bank teller, my family was adamant that a job at a bank was my best chance for success now that I had "given up" on my college degree. All summer long, I dutifully obliged my family—after all, what did I, a college dropout, know about success? Little did I know at the time, my search through Salem for a job that would please my family would lead me to a job that would satisfy me instead, a job that would teach me what it really means to be successful and would prove to me that I have what it takes to thrive.

I'll never forget the day that I stumbled upon the little bakery on a one-way street in Salem. I had spent the morning walking around the city, approaching potential employers and filling out job applications. My closest friend had come to accompany me that day, and by noon we had grown rather hungry and tired. Still, there was one last corner of Salem that we hadn't yet searched for a job opening, so we made our way across the downtown area, hurriedly walking along one of the city's main roads. Somehow despite our hurry, one of us noticed a small sign attached to the side of a building, reading: "A&J King Artisan Bakers." Wasn't this the bakery we had just been talking about? The one that recently won Boston Magazine's "Best of Boston" award? We decided we had to pause my job search for a bite to eat and a moment of relaxation at this bakery. As we neared the bakery's entrance, the smell of freshly baked bread mixed with hints of cinnamon and almond filled our noses: we could tell we were in for a delicious meal. Upon entering the bakery, we were greeted by a smiley server who took our order in a friendly manner and quickly delivered us our coffee and pastry. As we ate, we noticed colorful artwork drawn in chalk, depicting the bakery's seasonal offerings and the local farms that supply its ingredients—from butter to wheat to fruit to meat. To me the bakery seemed too good to be true—I loved baking at home, and I had a deep appreciation for how well the food was executed here, with the bakery's sourcing of local ingredients matching my ideal, benefitting the environment and supporting local farms by purchasing foods from nearby. By the end of lunch my friend was convinced that instead of applying to another bank, I should apply to A&J King Artisan Bakers; she successfully encouraged me to do so.

It felt like a stroke of luck that I found the bakery when I did. A position happened to be opening soon, and the bakery owners were looking to fill the opening as soon as possible; their job offer at the bakery came only hours before an offer from a local bank. I happily accepted the bakery position, but the anticipation of my first day at work brought back an uncomfortable feeling that I had avoided since withdrawing from school. Sure, my résumé and interview had impressed my employers enough to convince them that I was the right person to work at their bakery, but what if they got to know me better and it turned out that they were wrong? What if I made too many mistakes on the job? What if I was a fraud who had said the right things during the interview, but I was actually an incompetent employee? Thoughts like these had plagued me while I was a student, keeping me in bed when I should have been in class and preventing me from turning in my assignments; these insecurities were the driver of my withdrawal from school. As I arrived at the bakery for my inaugural shift, I noticed something that seemed peculiar to me—the most anxiety-provoking part of my shift was the anticipation of its beginning, not the actual work itself. Although my fears were not entirely diminished by the start of my shift, I had already learned my first lesson: for me, the hardest part of starting a task is the anticipation.

I hadn't worked at the bakery for long before my anxiety-induced questions were answered. I made a number of mistakes at work, from entering incorrect codes into the store's seemingly ancient cash register, to forgetting to forward drink orders to the barista, to leaving a piece of tissue paper (trash, by bakery standards) in a customer's bag of pastries. Surprisingly, however, neither my co-workers nor my employers took my mistakes as a sign of incompetence or fraudulence. Nothing I did wrong was catastrophic, and my mistakes were forgotten as quickly as they occurred; it became obvious that no one had the time nor the inclination to focus on my mistakes as much as I did. This realization led to a change in perspective and an improvement in my attitude. Instead of looking at my mistakes as personal failures and letting my worries stop me from taking action, I could look at mistakes as an opportunity for learning.

Over the next few months, I applied my new found perspective to all of my responsibilities at the bakery, and since I no longer saw the possibility of making a mistake as something to hold me back from trying new things, I began taking advantage of new work opportunities. Soon I accepted positions as barista and sandwich-maker. To someone who is inexperienced in food service, these jobs may seem unimportant and rather menial, but my experiences within these roles taught me a powerful lesson. At the start of my new positions, I often found myself overwhelmed. On busy days, drink and sandwich orders would pile in by the dozen; my movements were awkward and harried as I tried to complete each order. Determined to maintain my positive attitude, I persevered and over time I noticed that my movements became more like a coordinated dance than a series of jolted starts and stops. With a little bit of concentrated effort, I had mastered new skills.

As time passed, I became confident that I had the skills and know-how to attempt more challenging tasks. I took a leap and asked my bosses to consider me for a baking position. Even though I had no experience as a commercial baker and the transition from retail staff to baker was a major commitment in terms of time and physical energy, my bosses were confident in me. I was awarded the position of pastry baker and I learned a valuable lesson: opportunities abound, and sometimes all you have to do is ask. My time spent baking is also when I learned how much I actually loved working. When I was at school, I had worried that I would graduate only to find myself tied to some job that took away my free time and drained my energy, and I wondered about my ability to support myself. Baking taught me that work can be an outlet for creativity and a source of pride. I took joy in arranging a beautiful fruit tart or designing a new cake recipe. I got a thrill out of completing my tasks a little faster and better each day, and I learned that I actually could support myself. I just had to show up to work every day and do the best I could.

I loved my job at the bakery, but I was eager to see what else I could accomplish, and the day eventually came for me to move on. I had a few days left to pack up my belongings and move back to Amherst—my job had prepared me to finish my college degree. As I began my final bakery shift, I stood in the café area where I had eaten that first bakery lunch and took stock of the lessons I had learned while working there: The hardest part of any task is the anticipation. Mistakes aren't failures; they are opportunities for learning. Concentration and perseverance are all it takes for a once difficult task to become easy. I am more capable than I had previously realized. I took comfort in knowing that what I had learned at work could carry me through school, but I also knew that when the anticipation and the mistakes and the concentration of school life became overwhelming, I could find a delicious pastry and a few moments of solace at a little bakery on a one-way street in Salem.

Wake Me Up When September Ends

SAM GESUALDI

Gesualdi's meditation on place begins with a song. In precise prose that captures the wistfulness of one's first separation from one's place of origin, Gesualdi, with a balance of description and analysis, recreates an experience that all college freshmen are familiar with and that is also particular to him. Green Day's songs serve to provide a further context to the author's experience as they bring to the mind of readers how music and memory are closely bound.

August 14, 2015. 9:45 p.m.

Pulling out my driveway, I rolled down the window, plugged my phone into the car, and turned up the volume. The opening riff from "Welcome to Paradise," rebellious third-chord sounds produced by the inimical punk idols of Green Day, reverberated up the seats, down the steering wheel, burning with a physical, almost animal energy. I gulped and felt solid again.

This effect that music had on me is what made me seek solitary night-time car rides, particularly that summer before I left home for college. Until then, the geography of home had a unity of time: it held the present and the past. Until that August it was the place where I lived and the place where I was born and raised. But in the weeks to come, I would leave for college and then where I lived, the present would separate from the past. The present tense of the lyrics worked like a balm on this throbbing sensation. Within the finite space of the track, 3 minutes and 46 seconds, home is as clear to the singer today as it was when he first composed it in 1992. The seeming endurance of his clarity had so personal an appeal to me that I felt like recording the moment. So I pulled into a parking lot and took a selfie that I posted to Instagram, marking the moment with a precise date and time.

All I could think of in my final weeks of high school was graduation. We were a class full of fidgety seniors, bouncing our knees against benches as teachers struggled to keep our attention. College was to us as vague as the notion of paradise, pieced together from the parables we heard from college-going siblings: the dorms they lived in, the unmonitored freedom college afforded, the fun projects they partook of, the sports they played.

One afternoon, a friend whose brother went to UMass, where many of us were going, told us about this place he called Amherst Center.

"It's where all the cool kids go," he said. "You trek up there with friends Thursday nights and wait your turn to get inside. Around, like, nine or ten, that's when it gets really crowded, man. But you don't wanna get early either 'cause the cool kids don't do that."

"They grab pizza slices as they wait to get inside," someone else said.

"Inside where?" I asked.

"The post office," he said, and when he saw I was considering his response with some gravity, he added, "I'm kidding! McMurphy's. Remember the name. They go to drink n' dance—"

"—after they come of age," another friend cuts in. "Twenty-one. Remember that number as well."

He winked and placed his phone in the center of our circle. "Wake Me Up When September Ends" blared out of his headphones. He looked up and smiled. We thought he was alluding to our new lives as college students that would begin come September. What he knew but we didn't was that come September, he would enroll in the army and get deployed to Iraq. I don't know if it's true of the moment or if it's a detail I paint with the corrective hand of retrospection, but there was something gullible in his smile. It was as if he didn't feel like he was concealing something from us, the path he had set out on not real to him until after the fact, his flight landing him in a foreign country in the thick of a mission whose ambition would feel as foreign to him as the language that surrounded him.

August 14, 2015. 9:45 p.m.

In trying to figure what college would be like, I hadn't prepared myself for the immediate reality of leaving home. Like with my army friend, my departure only acquired the weight of clarity well after I knew the fact. It happened around a fortnight after graduation, when a packet arrived from UMass, and I read about my dorm: the building, floor, and room I'd move into. As I made a list of things I'd take with me to school, college became a process whose first step was a departure stamped with a date and time. And departure consisted of this room, my room, being emptied of its contents, one drawer, one rack at a time: an erasure, slow and definite.

I texted my friend Connor anxiously. "But we're gonna be back for winter break," he replied. I know, but those would be holidays, and so far we went to the beach for holidays, but now we're coming home for holidays, how weird is that: I did not say that.

Instead I got in my car and for a moment scrolled through my music library, wanting to hear something I hadn't listened to in a while, something that reminded me of my first years of high school. I was sixteen then. The distance between sixteen and eighteen seemed greater than two years. I chose Green Day's "Welcome to Paradise." I would listen to the whole album back then all the time. As I drove out my driveway, plugging phone to car, my experience of *relistening* to this song was different. When I first listened to it, the beat was its big appeal. But now the lyric sprang to life. As he sang, "To drive along these town lights," I drove past familiar landmarks—past people who waved at me before they saw me, who knew I was in the driver's seat just from the car and the hour. I *felt* what he meant when he says, "Pay attention to the cracked streets and the broken homes/Some call it slums/Some call it nice/I like to call [it] my home," even when my personal reality was different from the lyrical one.

When Billie Joe Armstrong wrote the song, did he know that in the summer of 2015 a teen in small town Massachusetts would listen to it, and in another time and another place, find in it his own meaning? It made me feel like I wasn't alone.

Growing up in that moment became to me this shift: it was my love for the song shifting from its beat to its lyric. It felt nice to tie the idea of growing up to a thing so tangible. In the space of a lyric it felt like I had journeyed the gulf between sixteen and eighteen. I was leaving home, and the song made it feel okay in that moment as I was driving down the road, illuminated by the passing street lights. I pulled into a parking lot and took a selfie to mark the moment. My phone buzzed with a text from my mom. I didn't read it. But I knew it was time to go back home.

In my first week of college what took me by surprise was not the newness of my room. It was the fact that I went from a small school to a campus so big it took fifteen minutes to walk from one class to another. On the third day of school, I stood at the intersection just beyond Southwest as hundreds of kids walked about me, the flow of traffic coordinated with handheld stop signs. I put in my headphones and tried to drown out my insecurities with music.

The sounds around me were blocked by Armstrong belting, "Seventeen and strung out on confusion."

It brought me the comfort of an intimate history, of the high school lawns where my friends and I hummed along this song on particularly bright fall afternoons. But rather than make me homesick, the song somehow sharpened my attention to the new buildings and faces around me, all ablaze in that sun-shine particular to New England Septembers. I sensed as if in my body there was an intersection between a moment past and the one present. I don't know how it happened. I didn't question it. I didn't know if my nostalgia was in the process of negotiating with my excitement for the new. Instead I thought, "What if a geographic separation need not translate to a gulf between the past and the present?"

This old song became a navigation tool for a new territory as I walked the street and trekked up the hill, towards my class, real time ticking alongside song time. September had far from ended. It had just begun. But in that moment, this sense of being present at once to what happened and what was happening made me feel like I was somewhere in the vicinity of waking up to a new kind of belonging.

Works Cited

Green Day. "Wake Me Up When September Ends." *American Idiot*, Reprise, 2005.

---. "Welcome to Paradise." *Dookie*, Reprise, 1994.

The Burden of Bliss

KATHLEEN KILROE

By using vivid language to bring Belfast's Peace Walls to life, Kilroe shows how a pivotal place can shape one's identity, asking what this locale can do to affect inner change. Kilroe's essay offers a personal reflection upon one's roles as a global and local citizen situated within broader reflection upon on the meaning of the Peace Walls.

In 1969, the Peace Walls were built in Belfast, Ireland, in response to the religious and political conflicts between the British Protestants and the Irish Catholics. In 1998, both the height and the length of the Peace Walls increased due to continued rioting and violence. In 2005, I stood in front of the Peace Walls, occupying a state of ignorant bliss. Ten years later, I am standing in same spot. I feel equally as ignorant, but this time, I am full of absolute shame.

It is early morning, and the sunshine leaks onto the compelling wall before me, standing 45 feet tall. My fiery brown eyes are pierced by a halo of golden rays. I feel a subtle trace of the fresh dew that remains as twilight finishes its routine retreat. Unusually, there is no gray this morning, a miracle for Irish weather. Instead, the clouds outline a sea of soft pinks and ambers, signalling to me that today is different. Across the brick wall, vibrant colors and street graffiti form sprawling murals. My eyes meet a skillfully crafted portrait of Bob Marley. The detailed figure is painted abstractly among his lyrics, fringed by splashes of green, yellow, and red. I am drawn to the signatures camouflaging the walls surface, an intriguing puzzle. Further down, I recognize an enlarged quote from Gandhi. The faded words "Peace is its own reward" are accented with pure, white doves, taking flight, creating a mix of the past and present, so beautifully mended together. Behind me, the noisy chorus of city traffic rushes past. The locals appear indifferent towards the sight. This overwhelming divide is just a normal part of their existence. They cannot see the wall like I do. They have known social conflict their whole lives, and I am just beginning to break the surface.

The concept of a Peace Wall feels almost shocking to me. After all, I am privileged enough to live in a middle-class home in an utterly average suburban neighborhood that exists far away from here. My idea of conflict is limited to parental arguments and breaking school rules. Real social, political, and religious conflicts are not within my realm. My life is a simple equation composed of a generic education, a subpar family life, and mediocre job. I never challenge this because "this" is all I know. I try to ponder the problems in the U.S., only to come up with unsure responses. I momentarily recall the last time I stood here, ten years ago, and realize nothing is changed. I am overwhelmed by my shame. A decade of time lost, and I am still just as blind to the world's disputes. At age eight, I was sheltered from the world's problems. At age eighteen, I have no excuses for my worldly ignorance. It's places like the Walls, ones of such cultural significance, that provide insight into the kind of person one has become. And in this moment, I know that "me" is not the person that I want to be.

I interrogate myself: am I that isolated? Oblivious? I conclude that I have wasted all 18 years of my life as a mere bystander. My emotions flare between outrage and disappointment. It is unfair of me to consider myself a member of society when I make no effort to be informed or active. Trying to overcome my close-mindedness, I zero in on the U.S. conflicts I know about vaguely. I reflect on racial cases like Michael Brown's, the upcoming presidential elections, foreign affairs, and gender equality. Although I am aware that these controversial topics exist, I truly don't *know* the details of them. My background had given me a sense of easiness and safety, and I abused it. A fatal mistake: allowing my naive oblivion to stealthily avert my experiences in adulthood.

To be "me" is no longer enough. I want, no *need*, to be more, to mean more, and to do more. I sat in the dark for so long that I forgot what it means to be in the light. But, as I face the wall with a renewed perspective, the light burns brilliantly within me. I refuse to remain oblivious, and instead aim to feel connected to the social problems around me. I now know that my isolated home, once seen as an advantage, is truly a burden to my growth. My concept of the "world" ended at the Franklin town-lines. Its safety and familiarity muffled any desire to see beyond my comfort zone. My perception of my upbringing has heavily shifted, similar to the transition of the prisoner in "The Allegory of the Cave" by Plato. My home acted as blinders, and now that I broke free of these restraints, I can embrace reality. Like the cave, my hometown was the only life I knew. I do not regret my upbringing because it is a key part of who I am now. Someone with an enlightened background would be impressed by the Walls, but being from a completely opposite lifestyle, I feel the urgency to change more than others. I cannot control where I came from, but I can control where I go. It has been and always will be my responsibility to get involved. I newly understand that I have a natural born role in society—everyone does. Anyone capable of learning about the world's conflicts should be inclined to do so. An individual is given one opportunity to make an impact, and it is foolish to waste it. Looking at the Walls, I no longer see just the beautiful art that I did before. I now identify them as powerful images and striking words filled with a profound sense of hope and the potential to produce peace. In a short time, the Peace Walls helped me recognize my own potential and find myself through purpose. In this moment, I never have felt so connected to the conflicts at home, even as I stand in a foreign country. As I leave the Peace Walls, I scribble my signature on the dark, worn brick. I look at my name, scrawled amongst thousands of others. It comforts me to know that I am not alone in my desire to be an activist and in my need to be a part of something bigger than myself. These signatures, all from individuals of unique backgrounds, are united by a single cause. I still know little about the conflicts I feel so attached to, but I am leaving ready to take action. "I will be better," I assure myself, "I will fight the darkness." I sign my name not only to represent my support, but also to accept a challenge.

Months later, I continue to act on my promise. Each day, I learn more about the world, and do what I can to make a positive impact. I joined organizations like CERC, MedLife, Relay for Life, and UMass Red Cross. Additionally, I keep updated on current events, and increase others' awareness. The escaped prisoner in the Allegory left his confined home, and discovered meaning in life. I am living the same journey, and reaping the same benefits. After my experience at the Walls, I am far more cultivated and open-minded. Even with major progress made, I have high hopes for the future and know more is to come. I can now look at myself, and say that I am genuinely proud of the "me" that I am.

The System

OLIVIA LAUGHLIN

Laughlin challenges the system in her raw and sincere Inquiring Into Self essay. She describes her personal experience in a style of stream of consciousness, yet at the same time she examines her thoughts with an academic lens. Notice her use of details and introspective depth and how she transforms it into an issue larger than herself.

I ran out. I barged through the crowd like I was chasing my dignity. I didn't even look back because everything that brought me into that place I vowed to leave behind the minute I entered. My hands were trembling, asking questions I could not answer. Who are you? The air was vacant, and I had never felt so empty in my life.

It was my first Saturday night at college, and I was surrounded by a group of people I had hoped to soon consider my friends. They were deciding on what to do with our night when the words I had been dreading stung the air: frat house. And the system was invited in. The system says that going to things like frat houses is how to have fun in college. It's the norm. And that comes with drinking and partying and dressing provocatively. So I had to change out of my comfy sweater and leggings. As I headed back to my dorm to get ready, I had goose bumps. But the weather report for a frat house was different. In an overcrowded room swelled with oscillating bodies, appropriate apparel would consist of very little if I wanted to maintain homeostasis, but more importantly, if I wanted to please the entrance facilitators.

I was never comfortable with portraying the sexy image society asks women to, but in that moment I wanted to be liked, I wanted friends, and I wanted what I felt I was denied in high school. So I followed the system. I put on more makeup and different clothing. I had to convince the frat boys that I was worth admission into their house. It felt morbid masking myself to fit into this perfect little mold for this cause. How strange, I thought, if I am putting on a mask, is my neighbor doing the same? And if so, does this image we all strive for even exist? Are we imitating something that lacks validity in itself?

These questions were swallowed by the system's grappling voice overpowering my conscience.

I looked in the mirror. I felt good, or told myself I was supposed to feel good looking like this. I was peering through the eyes of the hungry men that would scan me for eligibility to enter their beloved frat house. This was what they would want, whispered the system. I stumbled over my contradicting thoughts. This is what the stories tell about a stereotypical college life. But I forgot to question this life's morality.

The sidewalks were twisting with raindrops and weariness. The haunted sky mirrored the swarming thoughts painfully rippling in my head. I was a storm disguised as a sunset. The moon followed my Keds sneakers through the puddles hugging the valleys in the gravel. I felt the rain tapping my shoulders, flooding my eyes, soaking my shoes, giving me every reason in the world to turn around. I blocked it out and instead absorbed the voices of my peers, which were placid with confidence. Did this not feel wrong to anyone else?

We waited outside a square brick building with boastful Greek letters that sent a jolt of angst through me. If someone were to just look into my eyes, they'd see the screaming panic seeping through them. But instead, the guys in our group recounted our ratio, re-evaluating our chances of getting in. They conversed about moving one of the girls who was a little bigger to the back of the group because she would supposedly lower our chances. My heart dropped, and the pit in my stomach yanked harder. There was no spectrum; they wanted one thing, one breed from the system: one skinny, flirtatious, pretty, perfect girl. They instructed us to act tipsy, because we're easier that way; our power to say no is diluted. How appealing to those smug men, puffing their chests and wearing a drunk little grin because they call the shots while we desperately try to prove our worth to them.

As we advanced in the line, I noticed police cars strolling through "frat row," as they called it. Fear shot through me as I realized all the illegal and shameful things within my surroundings. Smashed beer bottles poked through the swampy grass. The flicker of a lit joint fell to the ground to be stomped on and put out. Clusters of people disguised their drunken bodies with sunglasses, forceful upright stances, and well-practiced poker faces. They were experts at maneuvering the rules. The house we were waiting outside of had black trash bags draped over all the windows. How clever; their secrets stay safe. How corrupted; their guests may not.

With the display of our most prestigious clones of the system's standards, we were let in. A city of grime layered the tiles that welcomed us into the house.

At the end of the hall, we entered a small dark room with music blasting. I looked to my right and saw a girl and a guy together. She was sweaty: her eyes were closed, her makeup disintegrating down her cheeks. She looked so empty, so powerless. Her body was limp, and it was offering itself up to the man. Looking at her was painful.

We travelled up to the second floor. There were four doors; all were closed. One opened as a guy spilled out of it, looking confused. He carefully closed the door behind him and fumbled down the stairs. The walls were blank, besides dents and black streaks here and there. Bugs made themselves comfortable—everywhere. Liquid dirt carried by shoes trailed endlessly along the floor. I felt the weight of the house. It was entirely invested and run by the system.

After only a few minutes, I made my escape. The frat boys guarding the house had a contemplative expression when they saw me burst out of the doors so prematurely after my entrance. I looked at them in disbelief. How can they stand outside of their "home" like security and evaluate each pleading guest on whether they are fit for entering their repulsive house of hungry men who want bodies and not beings? I wondered how they had fallen so deep into the system.

All my life I was conditioned to believe that I wasn't pretty enough, skinny enough, provocative enough, perfect enough. But for what? For this system? All for this deceitful, torturous system where men are programmed to hunt for one image of a woman? Because I don't want any part of that. So what if I don't fit into the system?

So why do we do this to ourselves? Why do we mold ourselves into this standard, when in reality it betrays our true beings? Women are shown Barbies and men are shown Superman and there is no in between. We give up our individuality because the system tells us there's one way to be loved, one way to look, one way to live. We look for approval in others to validate our worth. In this mess, the truth is lost. If we just stopped pretending that we're okay living with garbage bags over our windows and shields over our hearts, who would we be? We are not what the system brainwashes us to believe is right. We are a beautiful array of beings with souls to be loved unmasked. I was never meant to fit this image, and now I know I don't have to. It's time to question the stereotypical college life, the definition of perfection, and the frat boys scouting out desirable victims. It's time to question the system. Take off the mask, and break the system with me.

My Manhattan

BRIANNA PARKER

Parker's striking prose style and deliberate use of fragments demonstrate the power of individual words and phrases to evoke both images and emotions. Her selective use of detail and repetition communicates her particular experience and context while presenting New York City as a nuanced, layered space. Parker's essay showcases the depth of meaning that can be communicated in condensed form at the level of word, paragraph, and essay.

Timid. Collected. Indecisive. Independent. New York City, with its endless contradictions, breeds people with keen perceptions, impermeable wills to survive, enormous concern for one's neighbor. New York can be privilege; Manhattan suggests penthouses with skyline views and people glamorously hailing yellow cabs. Anyone who has ever listened to rap is immersed in a different kind of New York City. This New York is the backdrop for public housing. The ghetto struggle. Both New Yorks are real. They're not mutually exclusive. They coexist. I grew up in neither.

Being a generational New Yorker is almost rare. I am one. My dad speaks with a Brooklyn accent that most people think is just in movies about the mob. His version of New York is working hard, walking fast. A lot of curse words. My mom believes in the glamour of Manhattan: hailing cabs instead of riding the subway, buying European cigarettes for $14.00 a pack, shopping at four in the morning during Christmastime so she has the stores to herself. My sister's New York is sipping champagne with another guy who works on Wall Street, never husband material. Despite our thirteen-year age gap, both of our New Yorks were subway rides to school in kilts and knee socks. That was the outfit she wore when our neighborhood became a war zone in 2001.

It is no shock that witnessing 9/11 was traumatic, but most people assume a four-year-old would hardly recall much. I absorbed the entire event like a sponge. My preschool was across the street. I was supposed to go to the toy store in one of the towers after school. I saw the second plane hit. I saw stick figures falling out of the buildings. I heard bones shatter as they hit the concrete. Debris-covered adults screaming in sync with sirens that I thought would never stop. A burning smell that is ultimately death in odor form. My apartment ruined. A surgical mask over my face. One per family. Walking across the Brooklyn Bridge. Looking back. My pretty skyline. Gray. Blazing. Smokey. The sirens never stopped. An eerie quietness settled over the city.

Months later, all of the textbook side effects of post-traumatic stress disorder started to kick in. Subsequently, I began seeing a therapist on the Upper West Side. Every week, my mom and I would take the subway to W. 72nd street. We'd pass the Dakota building, where John Lennon lived and was killed. I sat in a room that smelled like oranges and played Candy Land. I brought my dolls and exhibited impressive maternal care. I told the therapist, Carol, about a "dust lady" that was following me around. She was trying to scare me. Out of one enormous atrocity, I chose to constantly relive a five-minute interaction my mom and I had with a debris covered woman in distress. She looked terrorized. She made eye contact with me. I could feel her terror. I felt her terror with me after that moment. After that day. After a year. After many years. Hiding in the crevices. In my dreams. While I was playing. My thoughts were governed by this woman's image. My childhood was plagued by her terror. My terror.

Therapy stopped. My life went on. Eight years old. Mute. Ten years old. Introspective. Twelve years old. Anxious. Fourteen years old. Self-reliant. Miserable. Therapy resumed. Same therapist. Four years. Kilt. Knee socks. Subway. At this point, 9/11 is not directly affecting me. I'm not mentally trapped by the image of a horrified woman. Instead, I'm empty and disappointed. I sit on the subway while businessmen and babysitters with children look at me as I cry. Another year passes. Still wearing the kilt. Still wearing the knee socks. I'm not miserable anymore. I am numb. I'm learning about myself. Sixteen years old. I'm a young woman getting over the suffering of a childhood event. It is history. It is my life. More time passes. More time spent sitting on the subway, looking out the windows into the abyss of train tunnels. Even more time spent packed in much too tight in a subway car. So little room to breathe. A lot of room to think. I sit on the couch on W. 72nd street. I stare at a vent. I speak to the woman that still remembers me as the poised little girl that played board games and took care of dolls. I'm early for a session one day. I sit in Central Park. It's like a scene from a movie set in New York. Holding coffee. Kilt and knee socks. Central Park is a fine place to think, I've decided.

I sit on the bench and I think how lucky I am. 9/11 changed New York forever. My New York. Everyone's New York. During moments where I failed to feel at ease in my own mind, I still felt comfortable in Manhattan. Train rides.

Central Park sittings. Walking down blocks and avenues for hours by myself. Relishing one neighborhood after the other. Independence. I recall walking in the Battery Park area to my church—a neighborhood full of construction and rebuilding. "They're saying the Freedom Tower will be finished in 2014." My dad said this to me. It was 2011. Fourteen-year-old me imagined 2014 as a shiny, bright new year in the distance. Seventeen-years-old sounded romantic and respectable. 2014 came. The Freedom Tower was finished. Time moved swiftly. Self-sufficiency. Self-knowledge. I possessed these things that are synonymous with being a New Yorker.

The traumatized little girl that I was needed the comfort of refilling metro cards, lit skyscrapers, and crowds of tourists in my way to heal. Compassionate. Carrying the stick figures I saw and the bones I heard forever with me. Carrying those people. Those people are omnipresent. They live in the street lights and sidewalks. They live in me. Aware. Perceptive. Tragedies happen every day. Somewhere in the Middle East, our country is conducting drone strikes. A woman in a hijab buying groceries gets a dirty look. A mosque is surveilled. People's place of prayer is compromised. Prejudice and ignorance are mistaken for patriotism. Those people carry the stick figures and the bones with them forever, too.

Those who have lost loved ones visit the memorial. Another tourist attraction. No Statue of Liberty or Empire State Building. This is somber. This is the sirens never stopping and the smell of death. Somehow, the day is now history. People travel from all over the country, all over the world, to see this exhibit. To feel the exhibit. This is my neighborhood. Preschool. Elementary. Middle. High school. Grocery store. Friends. Home. A headline. A live news report. A conspiracy documentary on Netflix. Graduating high school. Never wearing a kilt again. Never wearing knee socks again. Carrying the people who died. Carrying knowledge of who I am. My New York will never be a terrorist attack. It is complexity. It is empathy. My Manhattan is me.

Interacting with Texts

Preface

We often write to engage with the ideas of others, particularly in academic contexts. Because dialogue is at the heart of meaning-making in universities, *College Writing* asks students to "wrestle" with a published text in a unit called "Interacting with Texts." Writing to an academic audience, students work to balance understanding and fair representation of the text (specifically: effective summary, paraphrase, quotation, and citation of a text) with a critical response. This begins the process of writing to more distant audiences—audiences that are broader than fellow classmates, family members, or friends—and to understand the kinds of thinking and writing valued by academic communities.

The "Interacting with Texts" essays included here represent student interactions with the work of published writers. Drawing on their own histories and experiences, these student writers place their own perspectives in dialogue with those of a published writer. The challenge is, at once, to contemplate the sophisticated ideas shared by professional authors in the course's reader and to present one's own perspective on those ideas: for example, to re-think one's perspective on the topic, to apply a writer's claims to a different context, to tease apart the nuances of a writer's assertions, to re-define a key concept in an essay, and more. To understand these writers' ways of responding, we might imagine how the writers of the "Inquiring into Self" essays, based on their personal contexts, might have responded differently to the issues presented in this section.

Duty (noun): a Moral or Legal Obligation, a Responsibility

DANIELLA IANNUZZI

Iannuzzi provides a good example of a "conversation," combining a close reading of Sara Ahmed's essay "Why Happiness, Why Now?" with personal reflection. In the process, Iannuzzi complicates the idea of happiness by riffing off of the original essay in order to provide a deeper context for her own ideas.

Every morning when entering school, I would walk through the halls with a smile painted on my face, get my books out of my locker, and force myself to sit in the hall with my "group of friends." They would discuss the fun they had this past weekend mini golfing, going out to dinner, or whatever else they had done. I would sit and listen, having no input in the conversation. The girl that I would consider my best friend would say something along the lines of, "Sorry for not inviting you; couples only this weekend." And before I could show any emotion or reaction, I was saved by the bell. Everyone would enter homeroom, and the day would be about to begin. The problem for me was that it was only Monday morning, and even though so many people had told me, "Senior year is one of the best years of your life. Enjoy every second of it," all I wanted was for the week to fly by.

Throughout my freshman, sophomore, and junior years, I was always the one to make plans, include everyone, and have a fun time. Being happy came naturally to me. But during my senior year of high school, I had wondered why a time in my life that was expected to be one of the happiest was in reality one of the unhappiest times. Why was everyone else so happy and I wasn't? What was I doing wrong? In Sara Ahmed's essay "Why Happiness, Why Now?" I attained a framework for understanding why I felt such pressure to be, or to fake being, happy during my senior year.

Sara Ahmed begins her essay introducing her audience to a common perception of happiness. She explains the universal common goal that everyone has to be happy: "Happiness is consistently described as the object of human desire, as being what we aim for, as being what gives purpose, meaning and order to human life…. What they are describing is perhaps a consensus that happiness is the consensus. Do we consent to happiness? And what are we consenting to, if or when we consent to happiness?" (1). Ahmed explains how happiness "gives purpose" to people's lives. However, she puts this in question when asking if we "consent" to happiness, and if we do, what precisely are "we consenting to"? At the outset of her essay, Ahmed asks her readers to consider not only how they strive to be happy, but what life choices that requires them to make.

As individuals across the world desire and want happiness in order to feel complete in human life, it suggests the idea that happiness is an object that one can obtain, such as a bike or an ice cream cone. However, happiness is abstract, and therefore the path to possessing happiness is unclear. Even as Ahmed explains the goal of being happy, she uses words such as "perhaps" and "might" (1), suggesting that no one, including her, knows what happiness is and what one has to do to reach the goal of having happiness in their life. Because of this universal pressure that life "commands" one to obtain happiness (qtd. in Ahmed 1), it suggests that each individual, group, or nation has a duty to be happy. Each person should want and desire happiness, even if there is no clear path to how to obtain it.

Ahmed's consideration of happiness made me wonder why I wanted and desired happiness. What paths was I taking to obtain this so-called "universal goal"? Ahmed made me realize that during my senior year, I was struggling with the universal duty to be happy. There is an expectation, a duty, to find happiness. Ahmed claims the "demand for happiness is increasingly articulated as a demand to return to social ideals, as if what explains the crisis of happiness is not the failure of these ideals but our failure to follow them" (7). I began to realize as I was treated differently by my friends during my senior year, I had lost happiness. And now, I had to find it. So every Monday morning, I wanted the week, and the year for that matter, to fly by so I could find my happiness again and reach that goal. The methods to obtaining happiness are never questioned or doubted; it is rather the people who can't obtain happiness who are at fault. There is a "demand" for happiness due to the fact that it is a common goal and a duty. Blaming the failure of obtaining happiness on individuals rather than on social ideals makes me question what the world considers "society." If some, most likely many, are not obtaining happiness, even when following these social ideals, it would suggest that society as a whole is not obtaining happiness. Who is to say that the people who claim they have obtained happiness by following these social ideals are not making it up? Who is to say they these claimants of happiness are not lying just to say they have obtained happiness because they feel as though it is a duty of theirs?

I felt guilty during my senior year; I felt as though I was doing something wrong when I was not obtaining happiness. It is clear to me now that the pressure that is put on me to be happy is motivated by the universal duty of each individual to be happy in life. If you do not find happiness, you are a failure. I began to develop curiosity as to how society formed "social ideals" of happiness. What is supposed to make you happy? And for that matter, why is it supposed to make you happy?

As my curiosity grew, reading Ahmed's essay allowed me to discover the suggestions that the "science of happiness" has to offer as to what happiness really is. She portrays the notion that happiness is determined by certain situations and also promoted by others:

> The science of happiness could be described as performative: by finding happiness in certain places, it generates those places as being good, as being what should be promoted as goods. Correlations are read as causalities, which then become the basis of promotion. We promote what I call in the first chapter "happiness-causes," which might even cause happiness to be reported. The science of happiness hence redescribes what is already evaluated as being good as good. If we have a duty to promote what causes happiness, then happiness itself becomes a duty. (6)

Ahmed explains that in life, there are certain experiences that are supposed to bring happiness to your life, such as prom night, high school graduation, your wedding day. These experiences are being promoted by others, therefore making it a "duty" of theirs to suggest the fact that this certain "good" will cause happiness. But who is to say that the people promoting these "happiness-causes" are correct? Ahmed explains that while giving a place such a good reputation with high expectations to deliver happiness, the places are being "promoted as goods" (6). How can an abstract thing, such as a place, be considered a "good"? "Goods" is often paired with the word "service," the action of helping or doing work for someone. Perhaps people expect these "happiness-causes" to act as a good or service for them, providing them with happiness. This puts pressure on certain situations; it creates a "duty" for people to find this happiness service. Due to this, it puts pressure on those experiencing the promotional good to feel this happiness. This in turn creates the significance of "the happiness duty" (6).

I have finally come to a realization that the reason I was so guilty for not being happy during my senior year was because I felt a duty to be happy. Even though people around me associated senior year with being a great year in life, looking back, it wouldn't be totally inaccurate to say that my high school senior year was one of the worst years of my life. I was in a place where I didn't believe many people cared about me or my happiness. Forcing a smile through the halls was not something I was used to. As all of these people, young and old, were telling me to enjoy my last year of high school, I felt as though it was a "duty" of mine to be happy. I kept this to myself because I didn't want people knowing that I was unhappy. I didn't want people to judge me for being unhappy in "one of the happiest and best years of my life."

I was intrigued by Ahmed's idea of the universal goal of finding happiness because I never really thought about happiness in this light. I think happiness can be a very touchy subject for some people. If I had read this passage last year at this time, during my senior year, I think it would have affected me much differently than it did today. Honestly, I probably would have cried reading Ahmed's work. I think there are many times in life where there is a lot of pressure to be happy because you are "supposed to."

I have always been known as a very happy person. I am usually smiling and laughing. But that doesn't mean I am always happy or that finding happiness comes easily to me. After having read Ahmed's "Why Happiness, Why Now?" I will be more aware of when my happiness, smiles, and laughs are sincere and when they are forced because it is a "duty." And maybe someday when someone makes me mad, when happiness indicators do not live up to expectations, or when I just have a bad day, I will proudly show society the "duty" of mine to be unhappy for a little while.

Work Cited

Ahmed, Sara. "Why Happiness, Why Now?" *Opening Conversations: A Writer's Reader*, edited by Haivan V. Hoang et al. Hayden-McNeil, 2015, pp. 1–7.

Feminization, Education, Masculinity: A Response to Michael S. Kimmel

ANDY MARTON

Between the epigrammatic quotes that structure his essay and a distinctive voice that is all his own, Marton illustrates how to respond fairly to another author while making an original argument in a unique framework. Marton represents Kimmel's points without losing his own voice among the quotes. Rather, he extends Kimmel's points while testing them against his own experiences in high school, with family, and in his personal relationships.

Because there is very little honor left in American life, there is a certain built-in tendency to destroy masculinity in American men.
—**Norman Mailer**

In "'What About the Boys?' What the Current Debates Tell Us—and Don't Tell Us—About Boys in School," Michael S. Kimmel cites the statistic that boys "commit suicide four times more often than girls; they get into fights twice as often; they murder ten times more frequently and are 15 times more likely to be the victims of a violent crime" (91–92). His article examines why we have these disturbing figures. After reading his essay and reflecting upon my own experiences as a boy, I came to a conclusion similar to his: that boys in America are being trained with too much machismo that separates our "manliness" from our humanity.

Let's start with the claim that boys are being feminized. It sounds like this: in a world of political correctness and feminine idealism run amok, there is nowhere left for boys to assert their natural manliness and aggression. They're forced to act against their instincts, and the frustration of this unnatural abomination builds up with no healthy outlet for them. Kimmel rejects this idea by stating that it "creates a false opposition between girls and boys" (94). By arguing about why boys are so out of control, how they're neglected, we make the false assumption that girls and boys are completely different creatures and that there is nothing they have in common, an idea that Kimmel calls insulting (106).

I agree with Kimmel. Feminism has always been challenged, and its critics are willing to pervert it to re-assert male dominance. Reading Kimmel's portrayal of these arguments, I get from anti-feminist critics a call to return to the days where "men could be men" and women "knew their place," perhaps as docile housewives. I grew uncomfortable reading these arguments because they made me feel that women and girls are the enemy, the eternal yin to our yang, a force to be diminished. They didn't make me feel that women are human beings.

Having your adolescence at an all-male boarding school is just crap.
—Benedict Cumberbatch

This brings me to the conflict over single-sex education. If we accept the idea that boys and girls are irreconcilably different, then it seems reasonable to explore the option of creating schools for boys and schools for girls. It does seem, on the face of things, like an ideal arrangement. In my junior year of high school, I barely scraped by with a "C" for the year in physics because I took it with my then-girlfriend. I didn't focus, and we'd sometimes sneak out of the class for a while. It would be easy to make the argument that I would have done better academically in an all-boys school.

Kimmel rejects this idea. He asserts that "women's colleges may constitute a challenge to gender inequality, while men's colleges reproduce that inequality" (102). In short, men are taught that women are inferior to them because where are the women to say otherwise? Kimmel also declares that "single-sex education for women often perpetuates detrimental attitudes and stereotypes about women" (103). Essentially, these colleges reinforce gender stereotypes. One of my friends goes to the all-female Smith College, which is known for its liberal arts education, as is Mount Holyoke. Meanwhile, the very math-and-science based schools are heavily male. CalTech reported 65% of incoming students in 2013 were male ("2013 Incoming Class Profile"), and M.I.T. reported that in 2014 55% of those admitted were male ("Massachusetts Institute of Technology").

I, however, think single-sex colleges are more an effect of stereotyping rather than a cause; by the time students get to college, gender seems to have divided students on school subjects. According to the article, high school boys tended to list science and math as their favorite subjects, while girls listed the humanities, citing their genders as reasons why (Kimmel 101). Math is a "male subject" because it's concrete, while English, where there is no one right answer, and everyone is free to share various thoughts, feelings, and interpretations, is seen as feminine. It's easier to reinforce stereotypes about what subject goes with what gender when the boys and girls are kept apart from each other.

I have two observations about separate-sex facilities to add to Kimmel's. The first is that arguments for these facilities are rooted in the idea that everyone is heterosexual. Some estimates conclude that ten percent of the population—which is not negligible—is homosexual. They are not being served by a school that is supposed to take dating pressures away from them.

The other observation I had was that whatever problems men seem to have interacting with women (and vice-versa) are just that, problems. The answer isn't separating boys and girls because we distract each other. That's not how life works. Dealing with the opposite sex is a learned ability. I stated before that because I took physics with my girlfriend, I got a "C" for the year. Dating a classmate doesn't justify a bad grade. My dad (who married his high school sweetheart) was furious when I tried to make that my excuse. If there really is such a problem between boys and girls regarding how they interact around each other, however, then it's better to teach in school how to resolve that tension rather than to increase it. I'm convinced that single-sex schools do the latter, exacerbating this supposed rift rather than healing it.

Boys will be boys—Unknown (common expression)

So feminization isn't the problem. Coeducational schools aren't the problem. What is the problem? Could it be cultural? Could it be biological? Why is it, as Kimmel points out, that "few European nations would boast of such violent, homophobic, and misogynist adolescent males" (99–100), while the U.S. has all these scary statistics? I've grown up always hearing that boys are just like that naturally—they just normally lean towards aggression and violence. It's biological. Our testosterone just makes us want to run around, hit things, act "like a boy." But aggression is not biological or hereditary. Kimmel cites a study from Stanford that shows that testosterone "doesn't cause it [aggression], but it does facilitate and enable the aggression that's already there" (96). So, aggression has to come from somewhere else.

I've always thought it to be cultural. In America, we're bombarded with aggression and violence. Football is one of the most popular games in American culture. Our superheroes use their might to beat up or kill the bad guys. All of us are taught the basic "boy code" that Kimmel summarizes in the essay: don't be a sissy (I heard that one a lot growing up), fight to be in charge, and take risks (99). I don't know why in America we have such a focus on boys having to act like this. Or why it's encouraged. Whenever I got too rowdy or aggressive, or too macho (my parents' favorite word when I exhibited a bit too much of this behavior), my mother's first words were always, "Don't be a dumbass." She and my father always say that this need for aggression to prove how manly you are is stupid, especially when it results in games like "Flinch" that Kimmel describes (105).

Not only is it stupid, it's dangerous. Part of childhood is learning control. It's not necessarily a good thing when a boy is aggressive. The right response is to find better ways of channeling, not encouraging these feelings, as therapist Michael Gurian would have us do (Kimmel 107).

I attended Wayland High School, which, in 2011, underwent a serious tragedy. We had a student at my school who had always been aggressive and violent. He played football and was very good at it. Once in a while, he was known to have a violent outburst or a tantrum, but hey, what boy doesn't lose his temper once in a while? When his girlfriend broke up with him, he was upset, but he didn't share his feelings. Why would he? That's sissy stuff. The summer after they graduated, he brutally beat his former girlfriend and strangled her to death with a Bungee cord. He's currently in prison serving life without parole. But the most chilling part of this story is that everyone was shocked he could do this. Why? "Well, sure, he had a temper, but that's just normal." While he is responsible for what he did, isn't it possible that not encouraging violence and aggression in boys the way our culture does could have prevented this young woman's tragic death?

I'm not just a boy toy. I have feelings and dreams like anybody else.
—Jon Stewart

This quote highlights my overall point. The problem isn't that boys' natural aggression is being held back; it's that we live in a society where boys have this culture of "manliness" thrust upon them very early in their lives that's so unhealthy. I feel bombarded all the time with the cultural need to prove my dominance over other men, and especially over women. That's a sentiment that I find to be deeply harmful.

I could spend several more pages talking about possible sources for boys' aggression—abusive fathers, our media, fear of being perceived as gay, Freudian penis envy—but it doesn't matter. We know that there is some problem with boys when they murder, commit suicide, drop out, and suffer from depression at staggering rates. As we've seen, I reject the idea that feminism or coeducation has caused these problems. In fact, my argument lies in that both are good things. Growing up, we all (boys and girls) need to be encouraged to become human beings: good people who don't need to use violence to express themselves, who aren't afraid to show emotion at appropriate moments. Kimmel ends his essay with this declaration: "Feminists also seem to believe the outrageous proposition that, if given enough love, compassion, and support, boys—as well as men—can also be people. That's a vision of boyhood I believe is worth fighting for" (107). I couldn't agree more.

Works Cited

"2013 Incoming Class Profile." *Caltech.edu*. California Institute of Technology, admissions.caltech.edu. Accessed 4 Oct. 2013.

Kimmel, Michael S. "'What About the Boys?' What the Current Debates Tell Us and Don't Tell Us—About Boys in School." *Other Words: A Writer's Reader*, edited by David Fleming et al., Kendall Hunt, 2009, 91–110.

"Massachusetts Institute of Technology." *US News & World Report*, www.usnews.com/best-colleges/. Accessed 4 Oct. 2013.

Analizar Anzaldúa/
Analyzing Anzaldúa

LOUISE MONROE

Another essay that employs form to structure its argument, Monroe's reading of Gloria Anzaldúa uses bilingual headings to reflect Anzaldúa's own focus on border culture. Monroe's rhetorical analysis does not shy away from translating Spanish, and largely focuses on the pathos that Anzaldúa evokes. Both Anzaldúa's and Monroe's essays exemplify how writing can lead to a new understanding of the world and our place in it, particularly at places such as the borderland where language, space, culture, and history converge.

As young children we were taught that Christopher Columbus was responsible for our very existence. The United States would not have existed without his heroic efforts. Yet, around sixth grade, it began to let slip that that wasn't *exactly* how colonization happened. The happy picture of the New World settlers and the original Native Americans residents joining together as one in joyful unity was far from the truth. It wasn't as if the two cultures were sitting around the campfire telling jokes. The Europeans treated the Native Americans horribly, taking over their land and killing off their population.

This unequal partnership of cultures was mirrored in many places around the Americas. Westward expansion and the pursuit of "manifest destiny" led to the demolition of many cultures that were different from that of the expansionists. The current United States-Mexican border continues to be affected by the past terrors of the colonists and continued persecution by the United States. In her essay "The Homeland, Atzlán / El otro México," Gloria Anzaldúa creates an intriguing account of the history and personal struggle of the people who live on the border of the United States and Mexico. Perhaps even more intriguing than the actual story she spins is the way she spins it. Anzaldúa is an authorial powerhouse, commanding her audience to *listen!* "Pay attention to me," she demands through her rhetoric, a siren with a pen. Even though the piece is simply being read, it appeals to many senses and emotions. Auditory and memory skills, in addition to one's ability to read, are all called to attention. One is pushed to use all of his or her capabilities when studying this piece.

Escuchar/Listen

"El otro México que acá hemos construido el espacio es lo que ha sido territorio nacional" (39) roughly translates to: "The other Mexico that we have constructed / over there [in the U.S.] is in a place that was once / our [Mexico's] national territory." The "other Mexico" is the land the white people took over as they continuously pushed back the Mexican-United States border. The authors of this quotation, Los Tigros del Norte, as noted in Anzaldúa's footnote, are what is known as a *conjunto* band. Conjunto music originated during the 1800s in this border area that Anzaldúa knows so well. It has infiltrated both sides of the border to reach the people who are most affected by the barbwire. The music is a large part of the culture of the people; thus Anzaldúa chose to begin her essay with a verse from a *conjunto* song. Later she blends Spanish with English as she points out the dangers of trying to cross the border. "¿Qué dicen muchachos a echársela de mojado?" translates to "What do you say, guys/brothers, about crossing over?" (47). The answers they must entertain are not easy. The conversation continues, pointing to the great risk immigrant people take when trying to cross the border: the possibility of facing a coyote or dangers of another kind—having to depend on a drug or other kind of smuggler or being entrapped into cheap labor by "recruiters." The border is one without an element of safety ("Texas").

Both of these inclusions bring a traditional element of culture to the piece. Instances of culture which began and are dominant on the Mexican side of the border show that these people are their own people. They should be able to have a place to call home. They aren't just a smattering of nomads, all randomly brought together. They are a people who have persisted through generations, united as one, to maintain a culture they are so desperately trying to keep alive against the oppression of the white intruders. Their culture is as real as their struggle for survival. They are not simply the white people's throwaways.

Anzaldúa uses English and Spanish language throughout her piece. The text is created primarily for an English-speaking audience: the American people. Yet, the bits of intertwined Spanish are effective in proving her argument. The language strengthens the way she creates this border culture for the reader. In the first poem of the piece, she mentions "the sea" in English, yet in the next line refers to it as "el mar" (40). The inclusion of both shows how her culture, lands, even her nature are split by the "1,950 mile-long wound / dividing a *pueblo*, a culture, / running down the length of my body..." (40), as she refers to the border fence separating Mexico from America. Instead of calling the people originally from Texas, "Texans," she refers to them as "Tejanos," their true, original name. This border culture is one in which the white American people are dominant, and the native people are the subordinates. The balance of power becomes one of inequality, crooked. These people are reflections of the constant tug-of-war of the land, and the use of both languages presents an expression of this. The uniquely tragic cultural relationship between these two groups has been formed through the continual conquest and terror occurring throughout history. The border culture that has been created is strained due to one group's personal entitlement complex: the residents of the United States believe they are a superior strain of people.

The incorporations of Spanish language reinforce a stronger credibility to Anzaldúa as an author as well as adding to the strength of the piece. It adds to the realism that she actually is a person of border culture. As she tells how she has been personally affected by these misfortunes (i.e. her father had to switch professions from a farmer to a sharecropper because large corporations forced the end of dry land farming in the border area), one can more readily become a believer of the story and events that have taken place. The language hopscotch shows she is a person of both Mexico and the United States—that she is a child of injustice.

Escribir/Write

The poetry passages are arguably the best portion of the piece. Beginning with her own words, each passage conveys true emotion, adding to her central argument. By placing the poetry at the start of the essay, she can easily draw the reader in, an effective authorial technique. She chooses not to begin with an immediate attack on the white American counterparts who have made her and her people's lives so miserable. No, she chooses an emotional angle to tell her story. The words, "I stand at the edge where earth touches ocean / where the two overlap / a gentle coming together / at other times and places a violent clash," (39) lie within the first stanza. Soft words such as "gentle" and "touches" contrast with the "violent clash," as beginning descriptors between the innocence of the native people in opposition with the forcefulness of those who took over.

I believe one of the most compelling and powerful lines, not only in this poem but in the entire piece, comes a few stanzas before the end of this particular poem: "This is my home / this thin edge of / barbwire" (40). This statement epitomizes the whole inner struggle of these people. They have been pushed back and forth against the wire (figuratively and literally), too many times to count. Their home has become nothing—nothing, but a thin, sharp, cold piece of wire—strong enough to force the separation of the two nations and cultures. But most importantly, it has created a terrible sense of isolation. This isolation has made the people into a lower class and forced them to abide by the United States' pressure to stay within their boundaries. Their economy and way of life are controlled almost entirely by the white forces controlling their land. The people have become a product of this wire, weary and frustrated. The barbwire has become home. A home unlike any most of us will be able to imagine in our posh, easy lives. This is no land with a corresponding jingle confirming that yes, this land is my land, and this land is your land. No. These people have not felt such cheerfulness about their home in a long time.

Anzaldúa continues the essay by incorporating more poetry, but from other authors. These poems are further reflections by authors explaining, interpreting, and remembering the oppression of their people and the current border culture issues. This works as a technique because it provides more evidence than just Anzaldúa's own opinions and research. For example, author Violeta Parra is included: "El indio se cae muerto, y el afuerino de pie," remarks on the "Lost Land" of the Indian people: "The Indian falls dead, / and the outsider is left standing (43). The land is no longer one to call his or her own.

Recordar/Remember

Anzaldúa remarks on the history of the people of the land many years back. She describes the first people who lived on the land, tracing back to the roots of those who first called this place home. She chronologically describes each event which has led to today's reality: the battles, the economic changes, the unrecognized treaties, and so on. She relates back to the Aztec people not only by describing how they came to the border area, but also how they are believed to have arrived spiritually. She does this by inserting a small poem describing Huitzilopochtli, the God of War—"los aztecas siguieron al dios Huitzilopochtli," or in English, "The Aztecs followed the god / Huizilopochtli" (42). She thus incorporates a deep native cultural belief into her piece. After describing this folk tale, she starts an account of how Hernan Cortes and the Spaniards conquered the land and killed over fifteen million of the native people. By describing beliefs of an ancient culture and then paralleling it to the people who were ultimately responsible for the death and demise of many of the native people, Anzaldúa creates emotion. The current European views of the conquests are often thought of with pride: they gained land. However, through Anzaldúa's account, these advances are described not as a success but as a slaughter.

If she had chosen just to use her own opinions, the essay might be weak. By using factual evidence as well as other literary texts, she shows that she is not the only one seeing this as an issue—so do many other people. In addition to her factual evidence, Anzaldúa creates a very strong emotional piece as well. Her strength as a writer provides an argument so compelling, it is impossible for the reader to ignore. The combination of factual and emotional language and evidence create an undeniably strong essay. The techniques and strategies Anzaldúa uses strengthen her piece to perfect a mixing of pathos and logos to form ethos. The rhetoric is intellectually impeccable.

Work Cited

Anzaldúa, Gloria. "The Homeland, Aztlán / El otro México." *Other Words: A Writer's Reader*, edited by David Fleming et al., Kendall Hunt, 2009, 39–49.

Anger and Accountability in Antigua

ZOE SHENK

Shenk's essay is notable for both its incisive recognition and understanding of Jamaica Kincaid's forceful rhetorical choices in "A Small Place." Her introduction, initially framed as a critique of Kincaid's voice, catches Shenk's reader off guard for the rhetorical defense she later mounts in her essay. Shenk mimics Kincaid's use of second-person narrative as well as other rhetorical strategies not only as rhetorical analysis but also as a means to persuade her readers to recognize the truth of Kincaid's views.

In her essay, "A Small Place," Jamaica Kincaid creates an unquestionably powerful and provocative critique of the exploitive tourism industry in her native Antigua. However, by specifically targeting the privileged visiting tourists who perpetuate the oppressive power structure of postcolonial tourism, Kincaid risks losing her intended audience—those same people—entirely. Despite the danger, Kincaid masterfully walks that fine line between education and alienation in order to give us the rude awakening we deserve and require.

From the very first paragraph, it quickly becomes evident that Kincaid is on the offensive. You may initially think, as I did, that being from a tourist-infested, New England beach town lends you a certain level of expertise on the subject of tourism. Divorce yourself from these notions. Kincaid makes it very clear that *you* are the person under her microscope: "you are a tourist, a North American or European—to be frank, white—and not an Antiguan black" (111). As a tourist on a whirlwind tour of Antigua, Kincaid controls your every thought and punctuates each one with a jab about your abundant privilege and ignorance. When you note the beautiful sunny weather, Kincaid coos bitterly, "Since you are on your holiday, since you are a tourist, the thought of what it might be like for someone who had to live day in, day out in a place that suffers constantly from drought … must never cross your mind"(111). When you breeze through customs on your way to your hotel, Kincaid is there to explain:

> You are a tourist ... and not an Antiguan black returning to Antigua from
> Europe or North America with cardboard boxes of much needed cheap
> clothes and food for relatives, you move through customs swiftly, you
> move through customs with ease. Your bags are not searched. (111)

Every detail you notice about the island, from the mansions of corrupt politicians that line the poorly paved streets to the poorly maintained Japanese cars
that fill them, is twisted to illustrate the sheer magnitude of your ignorance.
By referring to the reader as *you* and writing in the second person, Kincaid is
able to force her readers to be accountable; she disallows readers from distanc-
ing themselves from their own problematic, ugly behavior.

Even the sprawling structure of the essay itself, while perhaps difficult on
the eyes, is extremely deliberate. Because Kincaid's intended audience is not
inclined to consider her argument in the first place, she forcibly silences readers by providing very few paragraph breaks. This manipulation allows for
fewer opportunities for interjection and protest by the audience. Even the
most hostile of readers has no choice but to go along for the ride, so to speak.

While Kincaid uses second person narrative and paragraph length to effectively implicate her readers, she does so at the expense of potentially being
perceived as accusatory. Overwhelmed by discomfort, it is easy to see how you
could feel personally attacked. You feel insulted, mocked, and unable to get
a word in edgewise by design. Kincaid uses a lot of sarcasm, which borders
on vitriol: "You needn't let that slightly funny feeling you have from time to
time about exploitation, oppression, domination develop into full-fledged
unease, discomfort; you could ruin your holiday" (113). She eventually loses
her twisted sense of playfulness and resorts to flat out insults: "An ugly thing,
that is what you are when you become a tourist, an ugly, empty thing, a stupid thing, a piece of rubbish pausing here and there to gaze at this and taste
that" (116). You can't help but wonder why Kincaid is so mean-spirited, so
aggressive, so angry. In your discomfort, you reduce Kincaid to a caricature
and transform her thoughtful, passionate critique of tourism into the ranting
of yet another Angry Black Woman. By stereotyping Kincaid as angry, you
are able to derail her argument and avoid engaging with the ideas she presents
in favor of critiquing her tone. This reaction demonstrates the very "tourist"
behavior outlined by Kincaid: the prioritization of your feelings and pleasure over the humanity and dignity of a less privileged person. Rather than
grapple with your own discomfort and think critically about your role in per-
petuating oppressive power structures like postcolonial tourism, you prefer to
dehumanize and dismiss the author. After all, you are a tourist. What is the
point of a vacation, if not to facilitate your unending comfort and pleasure?

By casting Kincaid as spiteful, you are able to return to your world of luxury and delight, completely devoid of responsibility or guilt.

To clarify, Kincaid's tone and risky stylistic choices do not ensure rejection by her target audience. Those who claim that Kincaid's unapologetically critical tone is not conducive to educating the reader fundamentally misunderstand the author's intentions. Jamaica Kincaid is not your middle school Social Studies teacher: she is not here to give you a sugarcoated lesson on the history of Antigua or hold your hand and help you cope with your guilt. Instead, Kincaid provides us with an authentic, emotional account of her experience as an Antiguan. In my opinion, this is much more valuable and impactful than a so-called impartial, objective narrative could ever be. By muting readers, Kincaid replicates the experiences of native Antiguans who are effectively silenced for the pleasure of tourists. Kincaid's perceived anger—whether imagined or real—only serves to further inform her audience about the condition of the people of Antigua.

Participating in this education is not necessarily an easy task. However, if you are brave enough to put aside your own discomfort and accept accountability for your privilege—to take the same sort of risk as a reader that Kincaid takes as a writer—you, the tourist, just might learn something.

Work Cited

Kincaid, Jamaica. "A Small Place." *Other Words: A Writer's Reader*, edited by David Fleming et al., Kendall Hunt, 2009, 111–116.

~~Dis~~connected

DANIEL SINGER

Rather than respond to Nathan Jurgenson's "The IRL Fetish" in its entirety, Singer responds at length to a specific idea, that of digital dualism. Through thoughtful analysis and examples drawn from contemporary art and his own usage of social media, Singer interacts effectively with the source text without losing his own voice as a writer.

"Have you heard the kind of things he's been saying?" said Veronda as she looked at me across our loud, sticky, break room that smelled of burnt soup. We had rarely spoken, and I didn't feel like engaging in a conversation in that moment because I liked getting my social media fix during my 15-minute breaks. So I shook my head and looked back down at my phone. But Veronda wasn't done.

"He's trying to build up a wall to keep them out. Get on over here, let me show you."

At that point I knew there was no way out of a conversation. So I went and stood behind her and peered over her shoulder, my eyes darting between my Facebook newsfeed and the tweets she showed me.

What shocked me about Trump's tweets, more than their tone deafness, and the fact that a Republican presidential candidate, no less, indulged a public forum in his racist and misogynist rhetoric, was the response it generated: followers of Trump retweeting and liking such material, and in doing so, bringing them into wider circulation.

I locked my phone's screen and sitting next to her we agreed that what would make Trump's presidential campaign historically relevant and active in public discourse even after the elections end are the digital footprints he's left on social media and people's publicly polarized positions on his statements.

Digital dualism, a term presented by Nathan Jurgenson in his essay "The IRL Fetish," describes the widely-circulated belief that either we are online, or we are not, we are either checking, or not checking Facebook. But, Jurgenson asks, are the two social spaces, online and real, mutually exclusive? In critiquing this notion, Jurgenson does not so much dismiss it as he extends it.

"Time spent online" means more than "less spent offline," Jurgenson thinks, and I agree, for what is "most crucial to our time spent logged on is what happened when logged off; it is the fuel that runs the engine of social media" (130). We post snippets from a lunchtime conversation with a friend; we Instagram a concert we attend in Boston. Social media apps like Yik-Yak localize and ground the nature of social media content, showing us posts from within a geographic radius.

Furthermore, where on the one hand, a cross-section of social media content is drawn from real life experiences, on the other, social media posts also shape real-life conversation. My conversation with Veronda is proof that "we live in an augmented reality that exists at the intersection of materiality and information, physicality and digitality, bodies and technology ..., the off and the online" (Jurgenson 130). What triggered my conversation with Veronda was her response to Trump's tweets. Her solitary experience, that is, shaped our mutual experience.

Not only do the real and the digital generate each other's contents, they also influence, according to Jurgenson, how we experience places and move through them. A summer on the beach with family and friends is a fairly familiar New England vacation story. What has changed over the years is the degrees in which we now experience it. When we walk the beach, even as we experience the moment—the soft, warm sand under our feet, the scent of salty sea breeze and fish dousing our breath, waves frothing over our feet— we consider how we are going to present the moment for digital digestion: An Instagram of the sunset? A Snapchat of the waves? A tweet about how much you're loving this experience? A Facebook post tagging the people you are with? Or better still, all of the above: it takes away the burden of choosing and reaches friends who're on one platform but not the other. In other words, we live the experience and simultaneously consider how we'll tell the story of the experience.

The desire to record something memorable and share it socially is of course not a new instinct. My parents took pictures of beach holidays and put them in a photo album that they'd show friends who came over. They would have small stories to tell about most pictures. What has changed are the cameras and the destinations of the pictures we take. The proliferation of smartphones has made it possible for anyone to be a photographer. And where before my parents sat with guests in our drawing hall, pointed at a picture, and told a story and received a response, we now leave notes and locate the place on our Facebook and Instagram maps, and our viewers respond with comments. Most notably, now we not only share photographs and thoughts but also witness other people share their very real experiences simultaneously—like multiple people sharing their photo albums in one digital hall. We may thus appreciate that the "notion of the offline as real and authentic is a recent invention, corresponding with the rise of the online. If we can fix this false separation and view the digital and physical as enmeshed, we will understand that what we do when connected is inseparable from what we do when disconnected" (Jurgenson 129).

The fact that we're thinking about how we share our experience does not necessarily take away from the immediacy or the intensity of the experience itself. Quite the contrary, Jurgenson believes that such an approach causes us to operate with a heightened awareness, thereby enhancing our experience.

Recently, the Museum of Modern Art (MoMA) mounted an exhibit of London-based artist Steve Cutts' work, sublimely comic depictions of our dependence on smartphones. The word "handheld," that so far has a functional meaning, acquires a new, disturbing connotation in these exhibits: one of his paintings, titled *Owned*, shows a smartphone walking a human who walks a dog.

My contention is that his paintings are not in conflict with Jurgenson's analysis. They are different parts of the same continuum. Where the painting's assertion ends, Jurgenson's begins. When we are not spending time digitally socializing, we spend time in social spaces from where we draw the material that we post online. What would we Instagram about if we did not go with our friends to the Boston concert—if the social occasion was entirely missing? We may check our phones when we walk our dog, but we also post a photo about something interesting we see on our walk, which might come up over lunch with a friend who's seen the post. Our times of separation and socialization are more interconnected than ever before. And, as addicting as the habit itself might be, it is one which we share with most of our contemporaries, and it is hence a good conversation starter. Even if what we do is talk about how terrible social media is. "One of our new hobbies," as Jurgenson points out, "is patting ourselves on the back by demonstrating how much we don't go on Facebook.... We have started to congratulate ourselves for keeping our phones in our pockets and fetishizing the offline as something more real to be nostalgic for" (128). Such habits and the nostalgia they stand for are the topics of active dialogue in social situations.

I acknowledge that our interaction with social media has opportunity costs—sometimes I walk into my class about five minutes early and find everyone's eyes fixed on their phones, and not wanting to be alone, feeling awkward to interrupt their engagement, I fish out my phone as well, when it would be better to use that time to talk and build community. And yet, consider this scenario: this morning, a friend and I shared an old joke, and because our friend, who was part of our trio, is now in Arizona, we made a post and tagged him in it along with a picture of us, the Southwest towers in the backdrop. He replied with another old joke we had shared and a picture of him outside the Arizona State library.

So I find that I am in agreement with Jurgenson that our new social behavior, codified by digital media, has created new opportunities of expression. It has allowed for a greater circulation of culture (photographs, videos, etc.) and conversations, personal and political.

"We may never fully log off," Jurgenson concedes, "but this in no way implies the loss of the face-to-face ... or the subtle appreciation of life sans the screen" (130–1). Social media has allowed us to develop a common language. As we talk about tweeting, friending, and filters, we are not connected more or less than before; we are connected in ways that are different from before, one that fits the diverse and complex social composition we are a part of.

Works Cited

Cutts, Steve. *Owned.* 3 July. 2015, stevecutts.wordpress.com/2015/07/03/owned/.

Jurgenson, Nathan. "The IRL Fetish." *Opening Conversations: A Writer's Reader*, edited by Haivan V. Hoang et al., Hayden-McNeil, 2015, pp. 126–31.

Adding to a Conversation

Preface

For the unit called "Adding to a Conversation," each student travels even further into a wider public audience by taking part in a larger conversation around a subject or issue that they find meaningful. What appeals to each student, what they find important and meaningful, has so much to do with their own histories and experiences. Students begin with a question, research multiple perspectives on the larger conversation around their question, and then imagine a potential audience that ought to hear more about it. Finding a point of entry where they can contribute meaningfully to this dialogue, students then write essays for a specific and more public audience—essays that include representation of and responses to sources but that are ultimately guided by the student's purpose. Here are essays that move beyond the "academic" world.

These essays are evidence of how writing serves the community. In the following essays, the writers bring their perspectives into the "world" and make their voices integral to larger conversations.

Plastic Bags, You, and the World

MILES BLACK

Black presents a scenario that every student is familiar with—the plague of plastic bag waste—and through detailed and careful research complicates our understanding of the issue. Rich with relevant examples and using a mix of popular and academic sources, the essay shows with remarkable clarity just how local choices can contribute to global problems. At the same time, Black offers suggestions that focus the audience's attention on potential solutions rather than needless cynicism.

It is a typical Monday morning: you have just hopped out of bed and are heading to your first class of the day. You are tired from a long, action-packed weekend, but you get a second wind walking through the beautiful college campus. The trees are full of color; the grass is freshly cut. But, wait, what is that on the ground? It is a plastic bag, one of the millions that fill landfills every year. So what is the problem with a plastic bag on the ground? Can't people just pick it up and throw it away? The problem is not as simple as the general public assumes it is. In fact, plastic bag pollution is a major concern that is not taken as seriously as it should be because people are unaware of its viral effects. Not only does this affect our own country, but it also impacts the rest of the world, including other countries and even the oceans. A single plastic bag that can be found all over the world can contribute to the death of livestock, such as a cow that could feed a family for weeks; prevent plants from growing by deforming and suffocating them; or endlessly pile up with the rest of our plastic bags in the streets and countryside. The entire world needs to make a change in the population's use of plastic bags, but we can start to make a difference here in our state of Massachusetts. Enacting laws regulating the usage of plastic bags in Massachusetts would greatly benefit our own environment and could create change benefiting the rest of the United States and other parts of the world.

Like many other forms of trash that pollute the planet, plastic bags accumulate at an alarming rate. Plastic bags can take between 20 to 1,000 years to decompose. There is not enough room in our country to dump all of our waste, and our country therefore sends waste to third world countries such as Ethiopia. Plastic bags are causing a major problem to the citizens of Ethiopia, killing one of their most significant livestock—cattle—and a single cow can sustain entire families for many weeks. The environmental scholars Velappagoundar Ramaswamy and Hardeep Rai Sharma notice a "sudden drop in milk yield and 75% reduction … incurring a heavy economic loss to the farmer. Losses or costs of several kinds occur like losses by death … losses of production … and the cost of preventive measures and treatment" (4). Living in a first world country, U.S. citizens are often blind to the effect we have on other countries. The impacts of something as simple as double bagging every time you go to the convenience store can ripple to a third world country and contribute to a major "economic loss" for a farmer in a country that is already struggling. If you think that is bad, further research in the article shows that one plastic bag can successfully kill a cow through either consumption of, or suffocation by, a plastic bag. Furthermore, food for cattle and other livestock is reduced due to plastic bags interfering with plant growth. The death of a cow can leave a family starving for over a week, all from one plastic bag. With the volume of plastic bags that our state uses every day, we have the potential to kill off thousands of cattle with devastating impact to third-world countries.

What can we do? Placing a ban or adding a tax on plastic bags in Massachusetts can make a major difference to the environment. Baggers at grocery stores and pharmacies mindlessly double bag items, even for very lightweight items. A customer's refusal of the bag or the double bag usually results in the bag getting thrown in the trash. In 2002, the PlasTax law was put into effect in Ireland. In a *National Geographic* article titled "Are Plastic Grocery Bags Sacking the Environment?" John Roach makes observations on the PlasTax law. He cites that, according to the director of Friends of the Irish Environment Tony Lowes, "just about everyone in Ireland carries around a reusable bag and the plastic bags that once blighted the verdant Irish countryside are now merely an occasional eyesore" (2). This regulation placed a 15 pence tax (roughly 24 cents) on every plastic bag being used. This did initially spark outcry by the citizens of Ireland, but people began to use reusable bags that could be purchased at any major store in order to avoid the taxes. This led to unbelievable differences in the "once blighted" Irish countryside, transforming it into the beautiful green fields in which the citizens make their living. In her article titled "Our Take: Plastic-Bag Bans," Katy Neusteter comments "[i]n Ireland, the 15-pence-per-bag 'PlasTax' has resulted in a more than 90 percent drop in bag usage" (1). Research has confirmed that the PlasTax has dropped 90 percent of bag usage, greatly reducing the amount of waste piling up in Ireland. Millions of bags are spared every year in Ireland as a result of the taxes, and the citizens are very happy with the status of the environment. Although Massachusetts is only a third of the size of Ireland, we would still be able to save millions of plastic bags from use every year. Having Massachusetts implement a similar plastic bag regulation to the PlasTax can make a major difference to not only our local environment, but also to the global environment.

American citizens typically complain about taxes: they hate to pay them and don't like what the tax money goes towards. At this point, one may think that a tax is the last thing our state needs. However, this practice has been used in various cities in California as well as Washington D.C., resulting in positive effects. The major concern that is preventing the movement to reduce plastic bag usage is the amount that should be taxed on each plastic bag in order to satisfy the citizens and still help the cause. On the one hand, if the tax is too high, fewer plastic bags will be used but citizens will be outraged. On the other hand, if the tax is too low, people will simply pay the tax and continue to use plastic bags. In D.C., Tim Craig observes that the "District's 5-cent bag tax generated about $150,000 during January to help clean up the Anacostia River, even though residents have dramatically scaled back their use of disposable bags." Judging from the success of this example, an ideal tax to place per plastic bag in Massachusetts would be five cents. However, the regulation should not stop here because if a tax were to be placed on plastic bags in Massachusetts, there would need to be somewhere where people would be able to purchase reusable bags. The citizens will be upset if there are no alternatives available at their local stores, leading them to grudgingly pay the tax and continue to use plastic bags, albeit in smaller quantities. This would be much less effective in helping the cause. If there is a tax that is placed on using plastic bags at stores, then stores should be required to sell reusable bags so that customers have the option to purchase and use them. There are many alternatives to plastic bags, including hand woven bags, thick polypropylene bags, or even paper bags, which can be recycled. Through these regulations Massachusetts can not only reduce the usage of plastic bags but also earn tax revenue that can be used to further improve the environment, which would be a major victory for our state.

When thinking about the idea of passing regulations on plastic bags in Massachusetts, one must consider the issue at a global level. Reducing our citizens' usage of plastic bags can save the occupation of a farmer in India, prevent an African family from starving, save the lives of living organisms, or even make the place we call home look more beautiful. It is realistic to think that there will still be people who pay the taxes and continue to use plastic bags on a daily basis, but the government can then use the collected tax money in order to fund environmental projects, such as D.C. did in the cleaning of the Anacostia River. Even if this regulation is not passed in Massachusetts, you can still make a difference. Consider a thought the next time that you make a trip to the store. Think about how easy it would be to take a reusable bag with you. Do you really need to use a plastic bag? With this simple change in your habits, think about how you can positively contribute to our environment and even save lives.

Works Cited

Craig, Tim. "D.C. Bag Tax Collects $150,000 in January for River Cleanup." *Washington Post*, 30 Mar. 2010, www.washingtonpost.com/wp-dyn/content/article/2010/03/29/AR2010032903336.html.

Neusteter, Katy. "Our Take: Plastic-Bag Bans." *Natural Foods Merchandiser*, vol. 30, no.7, 2009, p. 10. *Business Source Complete*, www.ebscohost.com/academic/business-source-complete.

Ramaswamy, Velappagoundar, and Hardeep Rai Sharma. "Plastic Bags—Threat to Environment and Cattle Health: A Retrospective Study from Gondar City of Ethiopia." *The IIOAB Journal*, vol. 2, no. 1, 2011, pp. 7–12. www.iioab.org/vol21spi1jan2011.htm.

Roach, John. "Are Plastic Grocery Bags Sacking the Environment?" *National Geographic*, 2 Sep. 2003, news.nationalgeographic.com/news/2003/09/0902_030902_plasticbags.html.

Unpaid Laborers Union

NICHOLAS FRAGOLA

Fragola discusses an issue that affects many college students in the country: the exploitation of student athletes in college. He argues that college athletes should be paid for their work and uses personal anecdotes and real life examples to prove his point. Fragola balances both anecdotal examples and research within his argument.

College athletes should be paid. The idea of the student-athlete, who plays a game s/he loves in order to gain an excellent education for free, is an outdated and inaccurate concept. The value that athletes provide their schools now far exceeds what they receive in return, especially as schools work harder to exploit the system and accept students for the sole purpose of being athletes. It seems the institution of college athletics has diverged from "student first, athlete second" to just plan athlete. Just ask my friend, Dean Adams.

The sun rises over Cowell Stadium, home of the UNH Wildcats, at around 6 A.M. By that time, Dean has already completed half of his two-hour sprint conditioning regimen. He will then proceed to spend another two hours in the weight room, and another few hours doing various football activities like studying plays and watching film. And this is just the offseason. As a Division I football player at the University of New Hampshire, a powerhouse program in the lower level Football Championship Series (FCS, or D I-AA), it is likely he will not sleep for more than 5 hours on an average day once the season actually begins. Football will be his full-time job, and schoolwork will unfortunately be secondary. His grades will surely suffer, yet football will always be the priority. His scholarship depends on it.

That is not to say that there are no instances of athletes finding success in both the classroom and in athletics. Cameron Fleming, an offensive tackle currently playing for the Patriots, graduated from Stanford with a degree in Aero- and Astronautics and applied to intern at NASA before joining the NFL (Thomas). Better yet, there are players out there such as Myron Rolle, who managed to graduate from Florida State University in two-and-a-half years as a Rhodes Scholar and entered an accelerated MD program at Oxford University, waiting a year to enter the NFL. But the three-time All-American, a man who managed to accomplish so much in both the classroom and on the field, advocates for paying college athletes for their work. His reasoning? He is lucky enough to be blessed with next level academic excellence in addition to tremendous, world-class athleticism. His teammates, however, mostly came from poor economic backgrounds; they struggled with schoolwork long before they had reached a college level, only being granted admittance to college because of their skills on the football field. Some struggled with basic reading and math. Rolle goes on to describe an average day, 8–10 hours of which could be spent on football-related activities (Southall 25). Those who make it to the pros are a select few, though it might not seem like it at Rolle's alma mater: there are currently 40 FSU alumni in the NFL, with more on the way. Even at a school like FSU, where their entire starting offense and most of the defense from their 2013 National Championship-winning team made the NFL ("NFL Noles"), the odds of going pro are still incredibly low. Consider that while there about 250 NFL draft picks each year, there are 250 schools combined between the two levels of Division 1 football, each team featuring rosters of approximately 88 players. In addition, the NFL is notorious for its low level of job security. In a sport such as basketball, where there are only 15 roster spots on each NBA team, divide those odds by 1,000, more or less. Essentially, players are promised an education they are not prepared to receive, nor does the university work to provide it. With players who already struggle academically spending such significant portions of their time on sports, it makes for graduates who are ill-equipped for the real world. They are putting in the work of a full-time job, and receiving none of what they are promised. They should be paid for their work.

NCAA President Mark Emmert would disagree. He uses the statistic of graduation rate to cite the value of a scholarship: "student-athletes competing in football at Division I FBS schools are graduating at a rate of 71 percent, and members of Division I men's basketball teams are graduating at a rate of 73 percent…. U.S. Census research continues to show those with a college degree earn $1 million more over a lifetime than those without a degree" (Southall 14). The problem with his metrics stems from the fact that those earning rates apply to all graduates; it does not account for those were handed a piece of paper in exchange for four years of athletics. All the while, the NCAA has profited off of merchandise sales, ticket sales, and media deals that players do not receive a cent of. The TV deal signed by Turner Sports to broadcast the men's basketball tournament is worth $11 billion, and does not include any of the 30 to 36 regular season games an average team plays (O'Toole).

According to Chris Smith of Forbes, ESPN is paying $470 million per year for the College Football Playoff, which totals four games. Schools receive millions of dollars from Nike, Under Armour, and Adidas for merchandise sponsorships. From this, students at Division I schools will get a few pairs of shoes and some clothes. Meanwhile, coaches like Nick Saban from Alabama make $7.2 million a year (Kerr-Dineen).

I offer only one solution: pay the players. One option is through direct payment from schools, but this could prove costly, creating even greater gaps in talent as schools such as those in the SEC take advantage of huge revenue streams to recruit the best players. A fairer system would be to simply allow players to profit off of their own names. Allow players to sign endorsements, charge money for appearances and autographs, and sell merchandise. This would eliminate cases of students receiving illicit benefits and would absolve schools of the burden of paying players.

Why should we care about this? For starters, if one were to ask a random college student "Should collegiate athletes be paid?" it is very likely that they will say yes, and there is data to prove this (Schneider 232). The average college student actually takes it a step further, believing that legalizing payment of athletes would significantly reduce the incidence of illegal compensation, one of the NCAA's biggest problems today. But aside from opinions, let us acknowledge the facts. College sports has become one of America's biggest industries. Every Saturday in the fall, millions of Americans watch college kids play the world's most dangerous game, and unlike the pros on Sundays, these kids receive nothing. Those brackets that people fill out every March? The spoils of free labor. Sports are a unifying monument in American culture; they bring people together. Students take pride in cheering on their schools. It is not fair for us as students to watch athletes be exploited. One of those athletes could be someone's son or daughter, or someone's friend. I can count a handful of friends who are athletes at the Division I level, and it upsets me to see how much they give and how little they get. They love their sports, and they certainly play for love of the game. But they sacrifice their grades and their free time and a normal college lifestyle in exchange for four more years of what they love. They are people just like us, despite the fact that their status as D-I athletes makes them seem larger-than-life. They deserve better. Let the athletes get paid.

Works Cited

Adams, Dean. Personal interview. 7 Mar. 2016.

Kerr-Dineen, Luke. "Nick Saban Would Be Insane to Leave Alabama for the NFL." *For the Win*. USA Today Sports, 12 Jan. 2016, ftw.usatoday.com/2016/01/nick-saban-would-be-insane-to-leave-alabama-for-the-nfl.

"NFL Noles." *Seminoles.com*. Florida State University Athletic Department, 27 Mar. 2016, www.seminoles.com/ViewArticle.dbml?ATCLID=209576821.

O'Toole, Thomas. "NCAA Reaches 14-year Deal with CBS/Turner for Men's Basketball Tournament, which Expands to 68 Teams for Now." *Campus Rivalry*. USA Today, 22 Apr. 2010.

Schneider, Raymond G. "College Students' Perceptions on the Payment of Intercollegiate Student-Athletes." *College Student Journal*, vol. 35, no. 2, June 2001, pp. 232–241. www.projectinnovation.com/college-student-journal.html.

Smith, Chris. "The Most Valuable Conferences in College Sports 2014." *Forbes*, 15 Apr. 2014, www.forbes.com/sites/chrissmith/2014/04/15/the-most-valuable-conferences-in-college-sports-2014/#2b1502cf774c.

Southall, Richard M. "The Pros and Cons of Making Major Reforms in the American Collegiate Athletic System." *Congressional Digest*, vol. 94, no. 6, June 2015, pp 8–31. congressionaldigest.com.

Thomas, Louisa. "Rocket Science." *Grantland*. ESPN Interest Ventures, 8 May 2014, grantland.com/features/cameron-fleming-stanford-nf-draft/.

How Chicken Wings Are Destroying Our World

STEPHANIE MACIOROWSKI

In this essay, Maciorowski addresses an often overlooked issue, the effects of raising chicken on the environment and human health. Notice how seamlessly she incorporates her sources into her argument as well as her use of pathos and logos, appealing to readers' emotions while developing a linear, fact-based argument.

In a world driven by convenience, poultry has come to dominate the food industry. Supermarkets are packed with pre-packaged or frozen chicken products. Butchers lay out cooked roasters for a quick meal at home. In fast-food restaurants, the majority of meals involve some form of chicken. McDonald's, Wendy's, and Burger King all have chicken nuggets, chicken sandwiches, or chicken tenders. For all the chicken that fills our bellies, we still find even more room for their eggs. Whether scrambled or sunny side, in batters or baked goods, eggs also provide a major part of our diet. From breakfast to dinner, we consume various forms of this simple bird. During the current health craze, to appeal to those looking to reduce their cholesterol and get fit, stores market "special" omega-3, low cholesterol, or cage-free eggs. Through both health perception and convenience, poultry has come to dominate our diet. However, what is the cost of producing enough chickens to support our ever-increasing demand for chicken wings and egg sandwiches?

Over the past few decades, poultry has come to supply almost "one-third of the world's meat supply and nearly all of its eggs" (Lawler 42). Annually, humans eat "almost one hundred million tons of chicken meat and one trillion eggs annually" (Lawler 42). While many consume copious amount of poultry for pleasure, third-world citizens in Africa and Asia depend on these birds to ward off malnutrition. Because chickens are relatively low-maintenance animals, people can raise them on small areas of land in order to provide protein in their diet. Examining only the food industry, we already require several billion chickens to satiate our demands. However, food is not the only reason chickens are raised. Flu strains are incubated in fertilized eggs, leading to the production of the world's 400 million annual doses of flu vaccine; without the ideal housing provided by the chicken egg, "one flu season could kill 50,000 people in the US alone" (Lawler 44). Who knew an egg saved thousands yearly? Poultry are also used for research, paints, printer ink, cushions, pillows, dusters, wine clarification, and insulation material. After accounting for all of these uses, we are left with over twenty-two billion chickens. That means every person on the planet could own three chickens (Butler et al.). Imagine if everyone on the street or at the gym was followed by three squawking birds.

Luckily, instead of everyone having their own personal chickens, the birds are crammed into production houses. In the egg industry alone, "there are approximately sixty-two egg producing companies with one million-plus hens," representing eighty-five percent of the total industry, and "sixteen companies with greater than five million hens" (American Egg Board). These statistics represent a transition to vertical integration in the industry. One person or company owns and coordinates the various levels of producing, processing, and distributing poultry. They could own everything from the hatcheries to the processing plants. In order to then maximize their output at each stage, producers incorporate economy of scale. Where there are fixed costs, such as for heating or land, producers will increase their units of output to spread out the price. If it costs the same to raise one hundred or one thousand chickens, they will choose the one thousand chickens in order to receive a greater profit once they are sold. Because of these prevalent practices, production companies have shifted to giant, conglomerate poultry houses.

Now we have over twenty-two billion chickens with the majority held by a small number of corporations. We can clearly see the damage caused by having large populations of humans together; look at the smog and environmental damage in major cities like Hong Kong and Los Angeles. Knowing this, what impact do large poultry corporations have on the environment? Poultry processing was found to be one of the top consumers and producers of natural gas resources, ammonia, carbon dioxide, and methane compared to all agricultural industries (Park 127). Several of these are known greenhouse gases that have been linked to recent climate change. In addition, ammonia has a direct correlation to problems in meat chicken production, including reduced growth performance and severe health issues (Zhao et al. 2). By grouping a greater amount of poultry in one location, the concentration of such gases increases to dangerous levels. This problem could easily be avoided by reducing the size of large-scale productions.

Part of the reason that poultry quickly rose in popularity was their ability to efficiently convert feed. All agricultural producers look to get the most output for the least amount of input. Over the years, chickens were bred to become the most efficient feed converters of all other animals. Most are raised and sent to market at over four pounds by forty days of age. With this rapid weight gain, sufficient feed must be provided. Laying hens also require sufficient feed and nutrients to support their continuous egg production. A study by Vamilson Prudencio da Silva et al. found that "the largest contribution to environmental impacts during chicken production ... came from the feed production stage" (229). Even without studying the air or soil, we can see an obviously greater draw on resources for larger groups of chickens. Based on this study, there is a statistically significant difference between large- and small-scale production systems, supporting the idea that small-scale systems have a lesser impact on the environment.

As more information about the risks involved with large-scale productions appears, there is a call for more organic, cage-free, or free-range production styles. However, these labels are not what one would picture. "Cage-free" only means that chickens are not confined to a cage. They usually live in aviaries, which are massive industrial barns that can hold thousands of birds, providing an average of one square foot of space per bird. "Free-range" is just as misleading; the label only requires that the chickens have access to the outdoors, not that they are actually outside at any point during their productive lives (Kelto). Organic chickens are more strictly regulated, as producers must conform to various USDA regulations. Such rules include being "free-range, fed organic feed, and receiv[ing] no hormones or antibiotics" (Kelto). While these systems may not be dramatically different from a caged life, they are still healthier alternatives for both the environment and chickens. Organic and other extensive types of production "can reduce the use of fossil fuels, fertilizers, and other inputs or have lower emissions from housing, and therefore can have equal or less environmental impact than intensive systems" commonly used today (Leinonen 263).

While it is clearly evident that there are better options for poultry production, there is little transition occurring. As of late 2015, only 8.6% of the total US flock was cage-free and 4.2% could be defined as USDA organic (American Egg Board). The majority of producers are left as large-scale, intensive systems. By continuing to call attention to the negative impact of large-scale production of poultry, we can hope to improve the welfare of the animals themselves and their effect on the environment. In fifty or one hundred years, we do not want our children to hear we destroyed the planet all in order to have chicken wings on Super Bowl Sunday.

Works Cited

American Egg Board. "Industry Overview." www.aeb.org/farmers-and-marketers/industry-overview. Accessed 09 Apr. 2016.

Butler, Keira, Tasneem Raja, and Maggie Severns. "Has the World Reached Peak Chicken?" *Mother Jones*, 2 Sept. 2013, www.motherjones.com/environment/2013/08/peak-chicken.

Kelto, Anders. "Farm Fresh? Natural? Eggs Not Always What They're Cracked Up to Be." *NPR*, 23 Dec. 2014, www.npr.org/sections/thesalt/2014/12/23/370377902/farm-fresh-natural-eggs-not-always-what-they-re-cracked-up-to-be.

Lawler, Andrew. "A World Without Chickens." *New Scientist*, vol. 225, no. 3013, 21 Mar. 2015, pp. 42–45. www.newscientist.com.

Leinonen, Ilkka, et al. "Predicting The Environmental Impacts of Chicken Systems in The United Kingdom Through a Life Cycle Assessment: Broiler Production Systems." *Poultry Science*, vol. 91, no. 1, 2012, pp. 8–25. *Oxford Academic*, academic.oup.com/ps.

Park, Yong Shin, et al. "Emergy and End-Point Impact Assessment of Agricultural and Food Production in The United States: A Supply Chain-Linked Ecologically-Based Life Cycle Assessment." *Ecological Indicators*, vol. 62, 2016, pp. 117–137. *ScienceDirect*, www.sciencedirect.com/science/journal/1470160X.

Prudêncio da Silva, Vamilson, et al. "Environmental Impacts of French and Brazilian Broiler Chicken Production Scenarios: An LCA Approach." *Journal of Environmental Management*, vol. 133, 2014, pp. 222–231. *Science Direct*, www.sciencedirect.com/science/journal/03014797.

Zhao, Y., et al. "Environmental Assessment of Three Egg Production Systems—Part I: Monitoring System and Indoor Air Quality." *Poultry Science*, vol. 94, no. 3, 2015, pp. 518–533. *Oxford Academic*, academic.oup.com/ps.

Saving Lives by Ending Them

MICHAEL MAGNANT

Magnant argues for physician-assisted suicide by eloquently employing pathos to convince his reader, using sources to persuade emotionally as well as to provide facts. Magnant's strength stems from using examples and disproving counter arguments in addition to his use of logical hypotheticals.

Matthew Donnelly loved life. But Matthew Donnelly wanted to die. For the past thirty years, Matthew had conducted research on the use of X-rays. Now, skin cancer riddled his tortured body. He had lost his nose, his left hand, two fingers on his right hand, and part of his jaw. He was left blind and was slowly deteriorating. The pain was unrelenting. Doctors estimated that he had a year to live. Lying in bed with teeth clenched from the excruciating pain, he pleaded to be put out of his misery. Matthew wanted to die now. His pleas went unanswered [by physicians]. Then, one day, Matthew's brother Harold, unable to ignore Matthew's repeated cry, removed a .30 caliber pistol from his dresser drawer, walked to the hospital, and shot and killed his brother. Harold was tried for murder. (Andre and Velasquez)

Physician-assisted suicide (PAS) occurs when a patient with intractable suffering or a terminal illness requests to end their life earlier than the natural course, with help from a physician. It can occur in several ways, the most common being taking a lethal dose of pills through ingestion (American Medical Association). This act is legal in four states of the United States and is in the process of being legalized in many more (Quill and Sussman). This issue is progressing far more slowly than others, such as gay rights or abortion, due to a heavy divide on the thinking in regards to this situation. I personally believe that physician-assisted suicide should be legalized. I believe that state-of-the-art palliative care—whether it be pain or symptom reduction, or mental health treatment—should always be the first option. But a patient who suffers from intractable suffering or a terminal illness should always have the right to end their life when they would choose to do so. The legalization of PAS would prevent gruesome situations similar to those of Matthew Donnelly and his brother, Harold, from continuing to occur (Andre and Velasquez).

California, Oregon, Vermont, and Washington are the only states where PAS has been legalized to date (Quill and Greenlaw). All of the other states are in the process of legalizing—or not legalizing—the procedure. Those who argue against PAS bring up thoughts and ideas regarding medical ethics, the preservation of life, and religion. Some bring up the point that death is not a controllable factor, that it is only determined by a God. So, with that point, they argue what gives physicians the right to "play God" in PAS? Take a deity out of the situation and a physician is simply doing their job as a healer to the patient. If the patient no longer has the will to live, or has a terminal illness that science has yet to find a cure for and wishes to decrease the intractable suffering of their deteriorating life, the physician would be acting as a healer to take away the prolonged death.

Furthermore, is a physician not "playing God" when they are saving lives as well? When an emergency C-section must occur or even when an EMT performs CPR on a patient, are they all not altering the natural plan of a "God" and changing the fate of what is supposed to occur? If physicians should not be allowed to "play God" by aiding a patient in ending their life, then technically a physician should not be allowed to "play God" when saving and lengthening lives as well, an idea that I am sure not too many people would agree with.

Other arguments against PAS say how the legalization of the act would devalue life. It is argued how with the legalization of PAS, the suicide rate would increase, and there would be a larger number of people ending their lives earlier than the natural course than if PAS remained illegal. The counterarguments revolve around data collected in Oregon as well as the fact that suicide is legal. PAS is a form of suicide that is and would be less tragic than the means of unassisted suicide that a person lacking the will to live would inflict upon themselves. Suicide is legal, so why should a less gruesome death be illegal? A lethal dosage of prescribed pills is substantially less traumatic than a bullet wound to the head or a noose around the neck. A person already legally has the right to end their own life, so why should they be restricted in ending their life, with help from a physician, in a more dignified manner?

The POLST (Physician Orders for Life-Sustaining Therapy) and Oregon Health Department have collected data on suicide rates since the legalization of PAS. It has been stated that:

> [S]tudies of the practice [PAS] in the United States suggest that in the majority of jurisdictions where physician-assisted [suicide] is illegal, it accounts for approximately 1–2% of deaths. In contrast, physician-assisted [suicide] is less common in Oregon, where for 10 years it has been legal for terminally ill patients who experience unacceptable suffering. Data collected by the Oregon Health Department show that the practice is stable and relatively rare, accounting for approximately one in 1,000 deaths. [0.1%] (Quill and Sussman)

This demonstrates how PAS rates actually decrease in states where the medical procedure has been legalized. This is most likely related to the entire process of PAS, where patients are first redirected to psychological or pastoral care, the level of their palliative care is evaluated by multiple professionals, and then—and only then—are they prescribed a lethal dosage of drugs. It is during this processing time where the patients either receive better care for their pain or symptoms, or begin to realize through the support that they receive how life is still worth living.

As stated before, I personally agree with the legalization of PAS. Although I do agree with the legalization of the procedure, I do not particularly agree with the practice of the procedure. I believe that PAS should be legalized, but patients with intractable diseases should be given proper care and urged to make the most of the last days of their lives, rather than end them quickly. I believe that—for the most part—life is worth living and that there are only the most extreme examples, as seen with the Matthew Donnelly case, where PAS would be a favorable means to an end.

This opinion of mine is shared by a former physician, Jeff Sutherland. I used the term former, as in he is no longer practicing, because Sutherland is living with amyotrophic lateral sclerosis (ALS), also known as Lou Gehrig's disease. ALS is a neurodegenerative disease that affects the muscles and motor functions of those who are affected by it. Once capable of treating others, Sutherland now can no longer move his own body, eat, drink, or speak on his own without aid. He can only communicate through moving his eyes. Sutherland believes that when he was healthy, he could never imagine living in the confines that he now does. But now that he does live in those confines, he is okay with it, and sees no reason to end his life (Sutherland).

The experience that Sutherland has gone through, and is currently living through, gives him a very unique perspective on the topic of PAS. The former physician lives in Canada, where PAS has been legalized (Sutherland). He was a former physician himself but now could even be considered a candidate for a patient receiving PAS. He does not want to receive PAS, however, and believes that life is worth living and should be appreciated regardless of current circumstances. Sutherland does not see the legalization of PAS as delegitimizing his choice to live, but rather has said, "Should my circumstances change [for the worse], I find comfort in the fact that I can now choose a gentle and humane death surrounded by loved ones on my own terms" (Sutherland). Rather than feel more obligated by the ability to end his life when he would want to do so, Sutherland states how he is even comforted by the fact that the option is there for him, a feeling that other patients in his situation must feel as well.

PAS is currently illegal, and there are without a doubt certain scenarios where PAS would be a favorable means to the end of someone's life. We are granted the right to life, and we are even granted the right to end our own lives. However, we are restricted in a physician assisting in the end of one's life, making it less gruesome and traumatic to all of those affected. Also, the process of requesting and applying to PAS has been shown to make the rates of suicide in general go down (Quill and Sussman). As the patient has to go through mental health professionals or pastoral mentoring prior to being cleared for PAS, they may reconsider their decision and realize that they would like to continue living once they receive some of the support that they may have been lacking. However, there are scenarios where a terminally ill patient is dying a debilitating, painful death in which PAS would be a reasonable option (Quill and Sussman). It is because of these extreme scenarios that I believe that PAS should be legalized throughout the United States.

The legalization of PAS will further advance the United States and continue its development of becoming more progressive as a whole. Individualism and the right to define one's own concept of existence has become more and more present, as seen through the legalization of medical procedures such as abortion and gender or sex reassignment surgery (Douthat). Yet because of the heavy divide and conflicting opinions regarding physician-assisted suicide, the legalization of this specific medical procedure has yet to occur in all states other than California, Oregon, Vermont, and Washington. Without this divide being settled, suffering people and patients will continue to search for a means to the end of lives, resulting in the persistence of tragic situations similar to that previously seen with Matthew Donnelly.

Works Cited

American Medical Association. "The American Medical Association *Code of Medical Ethics'* Opinions on Physician Participation in Abortion, Assisted Reproduction, and Physician-Assisted Suicide." *Virtual Mentor*, vol. 15, no. 3, Mar. 2013, pp. 206–207, journalofethics.ama-assn.org/2013/03/coet1-1303.html.

Andre, Claire, and Manuel Velasquez. "Assisted Suicide: A Right or a Wrong?" Markkula Center for Applied Ethics, Santa Clara University. 16 Nov. 2015, www.scu.edu/ethics/focus-areas/bioethics/resources/assisted-suicide-a-right-or-a-wrong/.

Douthat, Ross. "The Last Right: Why America is Moving Slowly on Assisted Suicide." *The New York Times*. 11 Oct. 2014, www.nytimes.com/2014/10/12/opinion/sunday/ross-douthat-why-america-is-moving-slowly-on-assisted-suicide.html?_r=0.

Sutherland, Jeff. "Physician-assisted Suicide from a Patient's Perspective." *Canadian Family Physician*, vol. 62, no. 2, Feb. 2016, p. 115, www.cfp.ca/content/62/2/115.full.

Quill, Timothy, and Bernard Sussman. "Physician Assisted Death." *The Hastings Center*. www.thehastingscenter.org/briefingbook/physician-assisted-death/. Accessed 26 Mar. 2016.

Texting and Language

EMILY SMITH

Smith offers readers a well-researched topic that uses a wide variety of sources to explore tonal ambiguities. By mixing personal interests and research, Smith deepens and enhances the essay's analysis. The end result is a nuanced view of the challenges of textual transmission in the 21st century as well as the history of abbreviated emotional communication.

"Hey brenda, can you help me w/ this essay? Thanks!! :)" After five minutes or so, Brenda texts back, "Sure." Brenda does not seem too pleased with helping me with my essay. What did I do to Brenda? I was so polite to her! I added a smiley face at the end of my text and everything! She could have at least written, "sure lol" or "no problem :)" to let me know that I was not being a burden. Instead, she just wrote "sure" with a period at the end of the sentence. Well then, Brenda. While complaining about Brenda, I realized that the smiley face and the abbreviation would have added a certain quality to the message that would have been difficult to decipher otherwise. It would have added tone. It would have added emotion. Instead, extracting the correct tone from Standard English turned into a guessing game.

The need to easily express meaning and emotion with writing has been around for longer than people realize. The linguistic particles—words that give contextual or pragmatic meaning—in text messaging and Internet language are more recent examples of using fewer words to convey the same message. However, they did not originate in these two mediums. Acronyms, for instance, were seen centuries back when "telegraph operators in the mid-nineteenth century used acronyms such as IMHO (in my humble opinion) and FWIW (for what it's worth).... Later, teletype operators used emoticons when chatting" (Goldsborough 64). "IMHO" and "FWIW" were both recognizable, shorter ways of saying an otherwise longer phrase, thus saving time.

People from various countries have also tried to insert marks to indicate tone easily. In 1899, French writer Alcanter de Brahm unsuccessfully attempted to coin a punctuation mark that would indicate sarcasm—a backwards question mark called the irony mark (Keats 125). To this day, recognizing sarcasm, excitement, and passive-aggressiveness among other tones in text is still difficult. However, recent developments for markers of emotions have been made, most notably in the form of the emoticon. The proposal for the standard smiley face in the US was first seen in 1982 by computer scientist Scott Fahlman: "I propose that the following character sequence for joke markers: :-). Read it sideways … to mark things that are NOT jokes … use :-(" (Keats 126). Eventually, the "joke marker" and its opposite found their way into mainstream messaging, especially in the early 2000s. Using other punctuation marks, many expressions such as a kiss :-* and a wink ;-) made their way into texting, with many "synonyms" attached with them (including =-), :-], and :)) (Keats 127). Emoticons took another form in Japan, expressing frustration ((>_<)), surprise ((*.*)), and secondary emotional signifiers such as blushing ((-///-)) and tears ((;_;)) in an anime-like style (Keats 129). Such features would evolve into modern developments around the world.

Modern developments include the use of emojis and abbreviations such as "LOL," along with different uses of punctuation to emphasize emotion. These features have become an important part of the quest to clear ambiguities in tone and emotion in colloquial writing. Emoticons and emojis, for example, have become representative of "tone of voice, facial expressions, and body language" (Goldsborough 64). Without emojis or emoticons, people would have to directly state their emotions (e.g. "I'm so excited!") or rely on the other person properly to properly identify his/her tone, which is fairly time-consuming and not as effective as using a single, distinctive image.

Abbreviations have also been heavily incorporated into text messaging for a similar purpose. A study by Baron (2008) showed lexical shortenings, or abbreviations, that were common in text messages included "ya" and "u" for "you," "prob" for "probably," and "k" for "okay" (154). These all reflect how people shorten these words in spoken language. Abbreviations have even tended to change meaning over time. "LOL," for instance, used to only function as an easier way to say "laughing out loud." It still carries the tone of laughter to some extent, but has evolved to functioning as an actual word. "Lol" can be used in sentences like, "lol, that's hilarious!" in which it is used to indicate laughter, and other ones like "lol I have to go now." Linguist John McWhorter labels "lol" as "a marker of empathy." For him, it is "a marker of accommodation" and "linguists call things like that pragmatic particles." It provides a certain amount of tone that makes the message less serious-sounding. Saying "lol no" has a different meaning than just "No." Texting, making up for face-to-face contact, utilizes abbreviations to match the emotion that comes from a person's voice.

Colloquial use of punctuation has deviated from Standard English in a way that makes tone more obvious to the reader. The use of punctuation is often exaggerated and unconventional compared to Standard English. In text messages, people will often end sentences with multiple exclamation points or question marks to emphasize excitement, confusion, etc., or separate sentences with ellipses to emphasize pauses (Kemp et al. 1587). Ellipses also indicate speech trailing off or are used as dramatic pauses (Baron 157). Since the receiver of a message cannot tell the sender's intention in regards to the length of pauses from a single period or the amount of excitement from a single exclamation point, exaggerated forms of those punctuation marks are used to carry a point across. Another example of unconventional use of punctuation includes the use of periods. A study by Baron evaluated sample text messages and IMs from students, which showed "seventy-one percent of all text messages and 65 percent of the IMs had no punctuation at the end of the message ... in messages containing more than one sentence, the students were selective about where they used punctuation" (156). Only in questions and exclamatory sentences was punctuation necessary. Periods were largely left out (156). Periods at the ends of sentences, especially in text messages, usually have a different, more serious tone and are used less by people in casual conversation. The use of a period at the end of a message is abrupt, leaving the impression that the sender is closed-off. In Standard English, it is proper to end with a period and use punctuation properly and sparingly; yet in colloquial text, punctuation is more prominent and emphasized, giving different meanings to common marks.

Emojis, emoticons, abbreviations, and punctuation are important in adding tone because they are used to mimic spoken language. Spoken language is effective in sending messages because of intonation, gesture, and prosody, or a sense of sentence structure based on tone; emojis and emoticons do this by mimicking facial expressions (Evans). Abbreviations and punctuation also reflect spoken language. In its overall structure, texting reflects the flexibility of spoken language. People do not worry about capital letters or punctuation when they speak, and they do not worry about them when they text; texting is essentially transcribing elements of spoken language (McWhorter). Abbreviations send a message in the time it takes to actually say a full phrase. Punctuation represents pauses and prosody. The grammar used in texting provides the intonation that most closely resembles natural, unrehearsed speech.

The flexible grammar and structure of texting is often mistaken as a sign of the death of language. Texting is far less formal than the language seen in books and academic papers. Too much exposure to the language of texting has caused concern for whether people will forget the conventions of written

English. There is mixed evidence of the effects of texting; some studies show that the exposure to texting has resulted in people making significantly more spelling errors, while others show no detrimental effects (Kemp et al. 1587). Emoticons and emojis have especially been scorned as "silly modern crutches" (Goldsborough). With each century, evolvements of language have been treated as the end of "proper" language. The concern has lingered for a long time, as one man from AD 63 demonstrates: "Spoken Latin has picked up a passel of words considered too casual for written Latin, and the grammar people use when speaking has broken down" (qtd. in McWhorter). Language has not died nor will it because of new grammatical particles.

Colloquial writing has not killed language, yet its usage does have some limitations. Emojis in their current form, for instance, only serve as particles of a language, no matter how useful they are. Despite representing certain ideas and feelings, and being compared to hieroglyphs, they are unable to be separate from language. Language involves having a wide set of words and expressions; emojis do not fill that semantic requirement, even with 800+ different ones to use (Evans). Vyvyan Evans notes that there is also a lack of grammar with emojis, and one cannot communicate complex ideas without referring back to written language. Other features of texting can cloud the meaning of a sentence if used too much. According to Goldsborough, omitting too much standard punctuation, spelling, and grammar, and using too many emojis can make a message too difficult to decipher. This is because it deviates too far from Standard English, making the meaning unintelligible. These emotional markers are also ineffective in business English, since a neutral tone must be used when discussing business or anything serious. Emoticons and emojis especially add too much emotion and are therefore considered inappropriate in these types of settings (Goldsborough). The language used in texting is useful in certain settings, and while they have differences in their use compared to Standard English, it does not make these additions any less valid to a language.

Texting has had a considerable impact on the way people write nowadays. People can more effectively convey tone through these new additions to language. Though the use of it is limited, the language used in texting offers to clear ambiguities in sentences.

I text Brenda again, asking if she wanted to grab some pizza later. She texts back, "sounds great :)"

Well I guess now she's happy.

Works Cited

Baron, Naomi. S. *Always on: Language in an Online and Mobile World*. Oxford UP, 2008.

Evans, Vyvyan. "No, the Rise of the Emoji Doesn't Spell the End of Language." *The Conversation*, 22 May 2015, theconversation.com/no-the-rise-of-the-emoji-doesnt-spell-the-end-of-language-42208.

Goldsborough, Reid. "Putting Your Emotions on Screen." *Teacher Librarian*, vol. 43, no. 1, 2015, p. 64. teacherlibrarian.com.

Keats, Jonathon. *Virtual Words: Language on the Edge of Science and Technology*. Oxford UP, 2010.

Kemp, Nenagh, Clare Wood, and Sam Waldron. "do i know its wrong: children's and adults' use of unconventional grammar in text messaging." *Reading and Writing: An Interdisciplinary Journal*, vol. 27, no. 9, 2014, pp. 1585–1602. *SpringerLink*, 10.1007/s11145-014-9508-1.

McWhorter, John. "Txting is Killing Language. Jk!!!" *TED*, 2013, www.ted.com/talks/john_mcwhorter_txtng_is_killing_language_jk.

Writer's Statement

Preface

College Writing ends with a "Writer's Statement," where students review their entire portfolios written for the course and harvest some of the most important insights they have discovered—about writing and about themselves as writers. By analyzing their struggles, their choices, their triumphs, they compare their past learning with their present knowledge in order to illuminate where they will need to go as writers in their futures. Learning to write well is a never-ending process, so this Writer's Statement is, in fact, a beginning that launches the student into the world of academic writing. They consider the various "tools" they have assembled in their writer's "toolbox": revision, responding to writing, reflecting on writing, writing for an audience and context, writing with purposefulness and the consciousness of crafting an idea into extended prose.

These following texts are the result of each student's unique experience of *College Writing*. They range from larger insights about the self and about learning to wonderfully pragmatic advice for any writer. We hope you enjoy reading about these students' journeys through *College Writing*, and the wisdom they gleaned as they worked throughout the course. Their advice and the insights they share serve as inspiration for us all.

Breaking the Silence

MICHAEL R. CABRAL

This well-crafted essay glides through each unit, showing readers how the course had an impact on this writer's process. Discussing the class, Cabral demonstrates what he has learned: the importance of audience, why context matters, what it means to have a conversation, and how his writing changed as a result of his participation in the course. The essay is very specific but at the same time offers universal examples that students can relate to.

In elementary school, I regularly received detentions for talking during class. This enforced silence left words swimming in my mind. I didn't find the outlet I needed until middle school: a notebook and a pen. My first attempts at writing were short stories and comic strips to make my friends laugh, my first audience. I then started writing love notes in middle school, essays as a freshman, and poetry as a junior. Then came AP English Literature senior year, and I reconsidered my love of writing. I longed to challenge myself as a writer, not just appreciate the writing of others; perhaps I was jumping the gun, but I've never been the patient type. I found this challenge in my first college writing course, English 112H.

Factors that I'd never before taken into account suddenly focused my writing, such as my relationship with the audience, my style, the tone of my writing. In the first essay I wrote for the class, "Why Write," I described what I had learned through my experience of writing a friendship-saving letter: "In trying to establish how I felt to someone else by using a pen, I achieved a firmer grasp on who I am as a person." In a reminiscent style, the essay brought out the significance of the event to me while informing the audience of my writing background. I learned the power writing can have, but I have come to find that writing serves an even greater purpose: it is a never-ending conversation with those before you, those with you now, and those in the future who will experience your thoughts. Since all people have different backgrounds and contexts, the conversation can take many different forms and can be interpreted in a completely different way depending on who is talking and who is listening. In this way, I was challenged to experiment with my own context while taking into account the contexts of others; in doing so my style of writing changed as the class went on, and I was presented with different challenges.

Starting with Unit I, I found myself excited by the opportunity to tell the story I knew best—my own. I wanted to tell the audience everything about me, but I immediately realized that without sufficient context, they wouldn't know what I was rambling about. Therefore, I took it from the top in the first part of the unit, discussing the cast iron pot my Nana uses that has been handed down in our family for generations. I told them about my hometown of Holyoke, my Irish heritage, and what it means to me by using a descriptive style including the smells, sights, and sounds of my memories. I used this story to relay the message that I'm an Irish Catholic who's proud of where he comes from and who demonstrates this pride in every aspect of his life. This pride is present throughout each of the unit's three parts. For example, as I touched on the process which "politicized me and motivated me to make my city proud" in the second part of the unit, "Lesson in Resiliency," I wrote in a highly motivated and persuasive style. I did this because the Holyoke school takeover pushed me to take action and trust my values. My attempts at using different styles of writing culminated in my creating a second-person piece about my track and field lifestyle coupled with my party persona, giving hints to the reader as to what was most important in the piece: my relationship with the coach, the task at hand, and the secrets that were being kept. The quote, "Match his enthusiasm; thank him for making these early morning workouts possible," was an attempt to reveal that the job was a metaphor for my track commitment, but I chose to leave gaps for the audience to fill in throughout the piece because no context is everything that it seems. I concluded the unit by taking on the biggest enemy in my context, my own conscience. At times, I had convinced myself that I didn't try hard enough. I compared my context to those of my competition and peers, and let them and myself know, by writing the argument out for all to see, that there is no right way of doing things as long as you're enjoying life. This first piece taught me a lot about myself and self-forgiveness, and that well placed stylistic techniques can make an essay more enjoyable and informative.

In my Unit II essay, "Finding Common Ground," I challenged myself as a writer and an individual to be humble and learn a lesson in front of the reader; whether that reader agreed with my original sentiment or not didn't matter to me. After presenting my personal advice to Chicanos to "stop looking at integrating into American culture as 'bleach,' rather as an opportunity," I put myself on trial. This critical style allowed me to present multiple ideas and opinions in order to establish credibility and allow for constructive discourse. The style of this essay allowed me to learn a lesson I didn't want to: that I was not sensitive enough to other people's contexts, allowing mine to get in the way too often when forming opinions. To be a true college writer, I needed to learn from this lesson.

For Units III and IV, I took my motivated style to another level by critiquing the process of school takeovers. "State (Mis)takeover of Public Schools" was an academic audience-focused paper that took my personal experience of being involved in a take-over and then matched my opinions with respectable evidence from multiple peer-reviewed sources. I found it challenging to compartmentalize my emotions to maintain my credibility, but I found a balance of emotion and facts led to a more enjoyable and informative style for the audience. For example, the quote, "Those sitting in their luxurious offices shame those who have lived through the struggles of their community for labelling their hardships as reasons for underperformance," points to the difference in socioeconomic status of those in charge and those in my community, but also points to the inadequate response to my community's demographics by those in charge. I took this point a step further in a different format when I wrote the Commissioner of Education, Mitchell Chester, a formal open letter in Unit IV. At times the letter was aggressive in style; for example, "The system you have put into place in Holyoke represents all that is wrong with the current education system in America," was a heartless attack on his record but necessary to establish my position ("Open Letter"). The style was changed from the formal, statistic-based commentary found in Unit III to a more readable, provocative, and persuasive work for the fight against state takeovers, all for the perceived audience of people reading the letter published in a newspaper, while also challenging the commissioner directly to change his policies.

Learning to change styles based on the audience was a balancing act, but I consider this growth as indicative of what it means to be a college writer. Finally tasting the freedom of adulthood leaves a college student with a choice: they can continue to learn and grow as intellectuals or fall through the cracks. To be a successful college writer one must take the strengths provided by what they have learned thus far, and then take it a step further; continue the conversation by participating thoughtfully, creatively, and respectfully, without fear and with relentless purpose. If done with proper technique and style, any true college writer can make an impact and break the silence.

Works Cited

Cabral, Michael R. "Finding Common Ground." Assignment, U of Massachusetts Amherst, 2016.

---. "Lesson in Resiliency." Assignment, U of Massachusetts Amherst, 2016.

---. "Open Letter to the Commissioner of Education, Mitchell Chester."
Assignment, U of Massachusetts Amherst, 2016.

---. "State (Mis)takeover of Public Schools." Assignment, U of Massachusetts
Amherst, 2016.

---. "Why Write." Assignment, U of Massachusetts Amherst, 2016.

Growth

AMROW HEGAZY

Hegazy's Writer's Statement is a meta-textual reflection on the act of writing. Using stylistic techniques such as fragmentation along with anecdotal examples drawn from his experiences in College Writing, *Hegazy displays both his process of learning and his ability to step back and articulate that process. By showing readers a specific text that he wrote for the class in its various stages of drafting, the author provides visual and verbal proof of how the process of revision truly helped him grow in his writing.*

It is a hot Tuesday afternoon, and the first day of my *College Writing* class. As I enter the compact classroom, I think to myself that it will just be like one of my high school writing classes that strictly focused on grammar and how to form persuasive arguments. I am confident that my soon-to-be classmates have similar thoughts. I arrive early just to be certain that I am in the right place. After finding a seat at the front, and placing the required books on my desk, I wait. Minutes later, it is 1:00 pm. Class is now in session.

Sunshine gleaming through the open windows. Birds' chirping—faintly ringing in my ears. I'm boiling in my seat. Unbearable. Fifteen minutes in, and to the rescue, our teacher asks us to go outside for a speed dating activity. With a sigh of relief I start making my way outside of the building along with everybody else. The whole point of the activity is to get to know one another (just as you would expect). We gather various pieces of information: putting down an adjective describing the last meal we had; the name of the last person we texted; our least favorite celebrity; three things we like to do in our free time that we wouldn't want anyone knowing about. It seemed trivial at the time, but this set the bar for what this class was going to be about.

The first steps are always the most important in bringing your words to life. I would start small and climb the writing process. Brainstorm. Outline. Write. Revise. I'd fragmented it so that I could step back and look at what I'm working with. This is who I was as a writer in high school. Yet as a writer in this class, I've juggled with two rough drafts that didn't connect with an audience, and sometimes I hadn't exhibited a powerful voice throughout. I've learned that my identity as a writer mattered. You can't emulate someone else's thoughts and ideas and expect to deliver something worth reading. You need to be original. Having finished the course, I've distinguished myself from other writers in class. You don't know who I am, where I'm from, or what I believe in. But by the end of this essay, you will know more of me.

2

Our first essay asked us to write about how what we do defines who we are. It paved the opportunity for my colleagues and me to establish a well-knit community. By getting to know each other inside and outside the classroom through our work, we had to learn how to talk about ourselves. In this essay, I siphoned the reader to a moment in my life:

> It was a calm summer evening when my high school friend Raheem and I went to the AMC Loews Theatre in Revere to watch Gareth Edward's *Godzilla* (2014). His mother had picked me up from home earlier at around 5:00 pm to catch the 6:15 pm screening. As we entered the Goliath of a cinema, we had to sift through the immense crowd lined up near the ticket booths. Laughter and voices were echoing all around us. It wasn't until we finally reached Theatre 9 where the loudness and crackling popcorn faded away. It was dim. Packed. We got to our seats and sat in suspense like everyone else in the audience. My friend turned to me and spoke about how he just loves dinosaurs and his passion to become a paleontologist to study prehistoric creatures. He was enthusiastic for this film. Dim lights slowly faded into pitch darkness. And so the movie began. ("Film and Television")

You are now encapsulated in my world. It's as if you were there with me at the cinema. You have a good idea of how things took place through the tone and mood I applied.

The use of visual narrative had an effect on how the reader would be able to understand what I was trying to say. This is a useful skill that I acquired in Unit I. The impact of forming words to create a mental image can have an implicit appeal to readers. This allows readers to go beyond just reading and interact with the text.

This experience influenced me to carry this prowess to my second unit where things really began to unfold. Our task was to analyze and interpret a text. Easy enough? Well, up until this unit I had not been fluent in this form of writing. To decipher someone else's words and make them relevant to me was something new. But that didn't stop me from taking my writing to the next level. I implemented what I had learned in Unit I to Unit II. How you might ask? I opened the essay with an anecdotal introduction that led to a full conversation between me and my mother. About what? My second essay was a response to "The IRL Fetish" by Nathan Jurgenson. We were required to interact with the text. Jurgenson argued that there is a misconception that being digitally connected corresponds to being disconnected from real life. How everyone in this society uses some sort of digital device. And what we do on these devices, with our exposure to the infostream, is a reflection of the world we live in. I responded in agreement in my essay, "Our Position Within the IRL Fetish":

> The infostream reflects what world we live in. Real world ideas, thoughts, and opinions are expressed. I follow politicians, celebrities, and activities I'm interested in. I like the ESPN page on Facebook because it reflects on my attentiveness to sports news. Another example is my following CW's *The Flash* on Twitter to be up-to-date with exclusive promotional videos; this indicates that this is a TV show I enjoy watching. "Twitter lips and Instagram eyes: Social media is a part of ourselves; the Facebook source code becomes our own code" (Jurgenson 2).

I brought my own context and connected ideas into this published text. The introduction I've mentioned set the foundation for how I use social media and how it is a representation of the real world. Contextual analysis and incorporating quotes and summaries were essential in this process.

3

Sharing our first drafts with our assigned peer review partner(s) was fundamental. This was something I personally got better at. Over time it became a tool for revision. For instance, I used the peer feedback I gave to my Unit II & Unit III partner, Sabrina, to self-critique my own writing. Basically, I took my own advice. You can see that relationship across the feedback I gave and in my writing. It's a reciprocal dynamic. The responses I received helped me strengthen my analysis and introduce a fresh idea in the conclusion that builds on to my argument. Because of this, I was also able to write a self-reflection letter in which I outline my revision plan.

4

Revision is central to my work as a writer. It's the determining factor as to whether or not my paper will succeed. Through my revision in the third unit, I was able to identify an audience I wanted to reach: young individuals who use social media as a way to express themselves. And I developed a strong voice in that essay that has the capacity to reach out to people with different outlooks on the topic I discussed. In the third unit I was able to successfully achieve a solid anecdotal introduction, interactive evidence, analysis, and a fresh conclusion.

In Unit IV, we responded to a different kind of text: film. We watched *Interstellar* and had to pick eight moments, then choose one of those eight moments to analyze the cause, effect, and consequence. This was also a piece of writing that exhibited deep analysis and close attention to detail. By now, I was used to this process. Just as I had done in my previous three units, I started with an anecdote:

> Upon returning to an older Romilly, Cooper was left in awe and possessed a hollowness in his heart after going through the pre-recordings his children Tom and Murphy Cooper sent him over that time period. At this point, Cooper was physically the same age as his daughter. Tears dripped from his blood-red face in such intensity knowing that he may never see them again. ("Interstellar")

Through my writing in this unit, I was able to find the causality in the narrative based on the moment I had chosen. I had to describe the scene objectively, the cause leading up to the scene, and the consequence that comes with it:

> The consequence of the pre-recordings led Cooper to finally reunite with Murphy on Cooper Station (a space colony orbiting Saturn). He was now one hundred and twenty-four years old, but had not physically aged but Murphy lay on her deathbed. With all her children and his descendants crowding the spacious hospital room, it proved to be a beautiful and an emotional moment. The narrative in this story is unique in the sense that what happens early on in the plot foreshadows what happens later on. Cause and effect happen across an entire storyline as opposed to there being an instantaneous cause and effect. ("Interstellar")

The foundation of this essay was based on it being a critical response paper. I ended the assignment by analyzing how the one cause I've chosen and its consequence built the narrative of *Interstellar*.

5

At some point, our teacher asked the class, "Have you ever wanted to say something, but didn't quite know how to?" We all raised our hands. *Everyone* was able to relate. This question planted the seed with the intent for us to grow. By the end of the semester we were able to sprout as more competent writers. All that we have learned in this class will apply to nearly everything that we will do in our future. To establish your own identity and guide your thoughts and ideas will push you to achieve great feats in the realm of writing. Wholeheartedly expressing yourself will make your voice heard and recognized as your own. I've made gruelling choices, especially in Unit II. Despite the fact that there wasn't a heavy amount of teacher feedback, what was highlighted for revision happened to be crucial to the structure of the essay. This prompted me to change most of what I've written, and successfully, without repeating ideas. Revision is the foremost important skill in the writing process.

***

Currently, with my hands firmly placed on my keyboard and mouse in my dim-lighted dorm room, I conclude in finalizing this draft. You now know more about me.

Works Cited

Hegazy, Amrow. "Film and Television." Assignment, U of Massachusetts Amherst, 2015.

---. "Interstellar." Assignment, U of Massachusetts Amherst, 2015.

---. "Our Position Within the IRL Fetish." Assignment, U of Massachusetts Amherst, 2015.

Jurgenson, Nathan. "The IRL Fetish." *Opening Conversations: A Writer's Reader*, edited by Haivan Hoang, et al. Hayden-McNeil, 2015, pp. 126–31.

Interstellar. Directed by Christopher Nolan, Paramount Pictures, 2014.

So You HATE College Writing?

MICHAEL G. MEZHBERG

Mezhberg takes his readers on a "cognitive roller coaster," as he approaches his Writer's Statement with creative experimentation of style. He is able to capture his audience's attention—other students taking College Writing—by catering the essay to them and addressing them directly.

Boring. Repetitive. Disgusting. Oh gosh ... how else could one characterize this freshman requirement?

Rewarding

Woah there, hold on a sec! Don't throw me away yet; I'm not finished. I know that I may have just taken you on a cognitive roller coaster with those dramatically juxtaposed descriptions of this class, but I did it for a reason. What is that reason? Well, you're still reading me. Somehow I got you to stay even after I totally dropped my shocking positive opinion of this class. This was the power of "knowing your audience" put to work—a very powerful skill to have. Just picture yourself in a situation where you are face-to-face with another person with a differing opinion. You know in your mind that you have an argument that will absolutely prove them wrong. But what good is that argument if the other person just ends up walking away from you? You may have had a strong argument, but your weakness lies in your inability to grasp this person's attention.

Strength

If you're an athlete, strength may mean full body strength to you. If you're a drummer, strength may mean having strong finger and wrist muscles. But if you're a human, a lot of your strength also lies within your mind. Just like working out for athletes or chopping out for drummers, learning is what improves your mental strength. And boy is there so much to learn! What I began to realize as I went through the *College Writing* experience is how mentally weak I was at writing. Let me explain.

I came into this course not really knowing what to expect. During the winter break before school started, I had an unfortunately non-foreshadowing conversation with my friend's mom. She had asked me about the classes that I was planning to take during this upcoming spring semester. I had mentioned *College Writing*. What did she say? "Oh, that should be easy for you, just a couple of essays." HA! Yeah right.

So that's how I walked in to *College Writing*, expecting the class was going to be easy and predictable. Then, on the first day of class, my professor told us to put our heads down on our desks. We were asked to think of a very small, seemingly insignificant memory that would randomly pop into our minds at the most unexpected times. In seconds I began to view this stupid old memory in my mind as if I were watching a movie. I never expected to eventually uncover a *goldmine*.

My first draft was very flowery and descriptive. Just to give you a taste: "The green grass dressed the scene in bright and vibrant colors" ("All Bogged Up"). At first, I didn't get the point of writing this essay. "Cool … It's just a project on vomiting rainbows onto a page and turning them into words," I thought to myself. As we began to expand on the first unit, however, I was tasked with finding a meaning behind this memory. Now, this memory is extremely familiar to me, but I always thought it was meaningless and useless! But through mapping out the timeline of events around the memory, I discovered something amazing: I value my opinions and I stand up for myself. This random memory was a turning point for me. It let me discover a "bond [that] let me grow past my parent's divorce, our suddenly moving from my home, my being bullied, and many other changes in my life" ("An Argument for Self").

What hit me is that I had certain channels in my brain that could not be accessed through any other form of communication other than writing. This may seem kind of weird, but it's true! Throughout my life I've never paid much attention to this memory. I passively glossed over it whenever it came up in my brain. Now I keep wondering how many other critical parts of my life my brain is glossing over. Writing helped me strengthen my brain's power of critically analyzing my memories. It feels great to know more about myself now.

Attention to Detail

Before taking this class, I would have never thought of writing as a conversation. At first that idea made little sense to me. Unit II (Interacting with Texts) began to clear up this image in my mind. I had read a text that I really connected with. It was an essay written by Peter Brooks that addressed the problems introducing standardized testing to assess learning in college. My first draft was a free write, and I was ready to spout off my fervent disapproval for standardized testing. In fact, I acted just like I would act if I was in a real conversation about whether a college education had genuine value or not: "Our wonderful politicians swooped in and solved the problem with no delay. 'Let's provide a standardized test to collect data on how colleges are educating their students!' Oh boy, how history never repeats itself" ("Unit II Draft 1"). I found that free writes were the easiest assignments because they were low-stakes and flowed easily onto the paper. They were never perfect, but they provided excellent molding material to soon craft a masterpiece.

What I had realized was that responding was much more than reciting facts from the essay that I read and simply agreeing or disagreeing. That way of thinking came from my high school days. No, no, no! My professor strictly warned me against the "five-by-five" essay, and those forms of responding usually correlate with this dangerous format. Instead, I extended Brooks' argument to show how standardized testing could lead to "the destruction of the future."

My Greatest Weakness

Unit III (Adding to a Conversation). My greatest battle during *College Writing*. At the same time, it was the most rewarding of the victories. I must admit that I felt very happy when I found out that the assignment let us choose our own topic to research. So I got into the library, and I didn't come out for a while. My topic was law enforcement, which I had picked due to my personal passion and future career choice. I was especially concerned about police misconduct, and I had some doubts about the body camera's functionality as the final solution to police abuse. I found tons of research material through the library website. It was extremely helpful as I began to learn extensively about the benefits and faults of the body camera.

The trouble I was having now was with developing ideas in my essay. Through the many conferences that I had with my professor, we had constantly identified areas in my essays where I just needed to develop my ideas more. For example, in my Unit III essay I began to reference a very powerful figure in the field of police rhetoric. Instead of developing his thoughts and connecting them to my solution for police violence, I just quoted him and moved on to a different idea, leaving that opportunity to support my argument in the dust. I realized that the process of thorough and continuous revision is vital to prevent the underdevelopment of ideas. By revising your paper, you will find ideas that may not be particularly relevant and are unnecessarily cluttering your paper. By erasing these, you uncover thoughts that need more development in order to be brought to fruition.

Pizzazz

I found Unit IV to be refreshing. I saw it as a way to totally revise one of our previously written essays. I was excited that we had the opportunity to choose from almost any writing format. With all of the skills that I had been equipped with in the previous units, I was ready to take this on with a bold approach. I wanted to create a very professional looking brochure that could really grasp the reader's attention and keep them flipping page after page. In my generative writing, I wrote that "I was fascinated by how marketers and advertisers use psychology and human behavior to sell their products" ("Generative Writing Unit IV"). I thought that my brochure was powerful and also achieved a similar outcome to my Unit III essay. This outcome was the exploration of something other than a police body camera in order to end police misconduct. I learned that multi-modal writing can reach far greater audiences while still maintaining the key components of a great essay: audience and purpose.

What about You?

Well look, I told you in the beginning that I thought this class was rewarding. After the late nights of writing and rewriting essays, doing peer reviews, and engaging in writing workshops, I feel stronger. I am more confident in my writing abilities. I also have discovered a new channel for my brain to communicate through. Through this channel, I could analyze and discover new things about myself and the world around me. So I want you to try to hear me out on this. No matter where you are in the course, if you're just starting or have finished, just do one thing.

Experiment

This class pushed me outside of my comfort zone. I was forced to experiment with different forms of writing and different approaches. After this, I honestly feel like a whole different kind of writer. If I was afraid of listening to my professor and trying out the crazy ideas and workshops that we had to do, I would have ended up with absolutely no progress and no urge to keep on writing. It's true that I want to continue writing. I actually go about my day and occasionally think about how great it would be to write about something I encounter. If you're having trouble getting started, here's a strategy that worked for me. Find the *exigency* to write. Write about something you *actually* care about. Take time to think through your generative drafts and initial workshops. This will help craft your passionate feelings around the assignment goals.

As for me, I'm off to write about many more things—and this time I'll be smiling.

Works Cited

Mezhberg, Michael G. "All Bogged Up." Assignment, U of Massachusetts Amherst, 2016.

---. "An Argument for Self." Assignment, U of Massachusetts Amherst, 2016.

---. "Generative Writing Unit 4." Assignment, U of Massachusetts Amherst, 2016.

---. "Unit II Draft 1." Assignment, U of Massachusetts Amherst, 2016.

---. "Unit III Review." Assignment, U of Massachusetts Amherst, 2016.